The Social Sciences and Fieldwork in China

Views from the Field

AAAS Selected Symposia Series

 Published by Westview Press, Inc.
5500 Central Avenue, Boulder, Colorado

for the

 American Association for the Advancement of Science
1776 Massachusetts Ave., N.W., Washington, D.C.

The Social Sciences and Fieldwork in China

Views from the Field

*Edited by Anne F. Thurston
and Burton Pasternak*

AAAS Selected Symposium **86**

AAAS Selected Symposia Series

This book is based on a symposium that was held at the 1981 AAAS National
Annual Meeting in Toronto, Ontario, January 3-8. The symposium was sponsored
by AAAS Section H (Anthropology) and was cosponsored by AAAS Section K (Social,
Economic, and Policy Sciences) and by the AAAS Office of International Science.

Published in 1983 in the United States of America by
    Westview Press, Inc.
    5500 Central Avenue
    Boulder, Colorado 80301
    Frederick A. Praeger, President and Publisher

Library of Congress Catalog Card Number: 83-50706
ISBN: 0-86531-644-9

Printed and bound in the United States of America.

About the Book

Following the formation of the Chinese Academy of Social Sciences in 1977 and the beginning of a Sino-American scholarly exchange program in October 1978, a small number of foreigners has been able to conduct fieldwork in China after a hiatus of over thirty years. Welcomed though these new opportunities were by potential U.S. field researchers, the initial stage of enthusiasm was shortly overshadowed by both the difficulties foreign researchers faced in China and the imposition, in early 1981, of a temporary moratorium on long-term fieldwork by outsiders. Sober without being pessimistic, realistic without being discouraging, the contributors to this book describe the context in which fieldwork in China became possible, the constraints under which foreign fieldworkers have labored, and the potential rewards of field research to both Chinese and U.S. scholars. They also assess the relative value of fieldwork in China versus fieldwork at its gate, Hong Kong. The book includes substantive reports by U.S. and Chinese scholars (among them Fei Xiaotong, China's preeminent social anthropologist) as well as concrete advice to those contemplating field research in China.

About the Series

The *AAAS Selected Symposia Series* was begun in 1977 to
provide a means for more permanently recording and more
widely disseminating some of the valuable material which is
discussed at the AAAS Annual National Meetings. The volumes
in this *Series* are based on symposia held at the Meetings
which address topics of current and continuing significance,
both within and among the sciences, and in the areas in which
science and technology impact on public policy. The *Series*
format is designed to provide for rapid dissemination of
information, so the papers are not typeset but are reproduced
directly from the camera-copy submitted by the authors. The
papers are organized and edited by the symposium arrangers
who then become the editors of the various volumes. Most
papers published in this *Series* are original contributions
which have not been previously published, although in some
cases additional papers from other sources have been added
by an editor to provide a more comprehensive view of a
particular topic. Symposia may be reports of new research
or reviews of established work, particularly work of an
interdisciplinary nature, since the AAAS Annual Meetings
typically embrace the full range of the sciences and their
societal implications.

WILLIAM D. CAREY
Executive Officer
American Association for
the Advancement of Science

Contents

About the Editors and Authors

Anne F. Thurston, *a specialist in Chinese domestic politics, is an associate in research at the Fairbank Center for East Asian Research, Harvard University. Formerly professional staff to the China programs of the Social Science Research Council in New York City, she also served as staff to a delegation to China of scholars representing the Joint Committee on Contemporary China (of the Social Science Research Council and the American Council of Learned Societies) and the Committee on the Studies of Chinese Civilization (of the ACLS). In 1981-82 she spent nine months in China conducting research on the victims of China's Cultural Revolution. She coedited* Humanistic and Social Science Research in China *(with J. Parker; New York: Social Science Research Council, 1980).*

Burton Pasternak *is professor of anthropology at Hunter College, City University of New York. He has served as chairman of the Joint Committee on Contemporary China and was a member of the Committee on Scholarly Communication with the People's Republic of China's Committee on Advanced Study in China. In 1981-82 he spent six months in Tianjin, China, conducting demographic research. He has also done social demographic studies in rural Taiwan and is the author of* Kinship and Community in Two Chinese Villages *(Stanford University Press, 1972),* Introduction to Kinship and Social Organization *(Prentice-Hall, 1976), and* Guests in the Dragon: Social Demography of a Chinese District *(Columbia University Press, in press).*

Steven B. Butler, *a political scientist and fellow of the Institute of Current World Affairs based in Hanover, New Hampshire, is currently living and traveling in Asia. He conducted field research in a Chinese village in 1980 on a grant from the Committee on Scholarly Communication with the*

People's Republic of China and has just completed a book on China's rural budgetary and administrative system.

Norma Diamond, *professor of anthropology at the University of Michigan, has specialized in ethnology and economic anthropology. She has written on the ethnography of East Asia, the status of women in Taiwan, and economic development and government policies in the People's Republic of China. In 1979-80 she was visiting professor at Shandong University in Jinan, China, and conducted field research in Taitou village, Shandong. She is the author of* K'un Shen: A Taiwan Village *(Holt Rinehart Winston, 1969) and is a member of the editorial board of* Modern China.

Helen Fung-har Siu, *a specialist in economic anthropology and peasant societies, is assistant professor of anthropology at Yale University. She conducted periodic field research in China from 1974 to 1982 and has written on rural leadership and socialist transformation in the PRC, rural industrialization, and contemporary Chinese literature. She is coeditor of* Mao's Harvest: Voices from China's New Generation *(with Z. Stern; Oxford University Press, 1983) and is currently at work on another manuscript, "Economic Development and Institutional Change in a Chinese Commune."*

Martin King Whyte *is professor of sociology at the University of Michigan, Ann Arbor. His research interests are comparative sociology, sociology of the family, and contemporary China. A former director of the Universities Service Centre in Hong Kong, he was a member of the Social Science Research Council's Joint Committee on Contemporary China and the China and Inner Asia Council of the Association for Asian Studies. His publications include* Small Groups and Political Rituals in China *(University of California Press, 1974) and* Village and Family in Contemporary China *and* Urban Life in Contemporary China *(both with W. Parish; University of Chicago Press, 1978 and 1983, respectively).*

Fei Xiaotong, *China's preeminent social anthropologist, is director of the Institute of Sociology at the Chinese Academy of Social Sciences in Peking and Vice Chairman of the Chinese People's Political Consultative Congress. Recipient of the Malinowski Award from the Society for Applied Anthropology and the Huxley Award from the Royal Anthropological Institute of Great Britain, he was educated at Qinghua University and the London School of Economics. He has conducted field research on the Yao national minorities in Guangxi province and in Kaixiangong village in the Yangtze region. He is author of* Peasant Life in China *(London: Routledge & Kegan Paul, 1939) and* Earthbound China *and* China's Gentry *(University of Chicago Press, 1945 and 1953, respectively).*

Preface

    This volume is the product of a panel on Sino-American exchanges in the social sciences presented at the annual meeting of the American Association for the Advancement of Science held in Toronto, Canada, in January 1981. A major purpose of the panel was to examine the possibilities within China of social science fieldwork--possibilities for "deep immersion" by outsiders in Chinese life, "intimate participation in a community and observation of modes of behavior and the organization of social life"[1] for sustained periods of time. Focusing on the structure of social science exchanges and on the relationship between the revitalization of sociology and anthropology--the two social science disciplines most dependent upon field research--and the possibilities for fieldwork in China, the panel also included reports from several of the first Americans to have conducted field research in China in some 30 years.

    Since that panel was held, the possibilities for conducting fieldwork in China have contracted. While Chinese authorities continue to permit short-term visits to select field sites, a moratorium on long-term participant observation is now in effect.

    At several points between the panel presentations and the final editing of this volume, we have questioned the merit of publishing a volume on fieldwork in China at a time when long-term fieldwork by outsiders is no longer permitted. Repeatedly, both we, the editorial staff at the American Association for the Advancement of Science, and colleagues with whom we have discussed this dilemma, have concluded that the volume must proceed. Above all, the moratorium does not

---

1. Roger M. Keesing, *Cultural Anthropology: A Contemporary Perspective* (New York: Holt, Rinehart and Winston, 1981), pp. 5-6.

detract from the very valuable contributions of those few who were able to conduct field research before its imposition. Moreover, the status of Sino-American exchanges in the social sciences can be expected to remain fluid for some time to come. To wait until the situation stabilizes and new patterns of exchange emerge would both deny the contributions of those who have already conducted research and prevent others who may go to the field later from learning from the experience of those who have paved the way. We therefore decided to proceed, and the reports from the field contained within this volume remain essentially as they were presented at the panel, edited only for clarity and greater comparability.

The contributions by the two editors reflect our current understanding of both the contraction of fieldwork possibilities and the current uncertainty of exchanges in the social sciences. By drawing on our own experiences in China and the experiences of other contributors, we have tried both to confront readers with many of the dilemmas that future fieldworkers are also likely to face and to suggest the rewards that can be reaped even when painful compromises must be made.

When Professor Fei Xiaotong, China's noted social anthropologist and currently Director of the Institute of Sociology at the Chinese Academy of Social Sciences, spoke at the panel, his discussion focused on the revival of sociology in China. In the process of editing the volume, however, we felt that there was considerable overlap between Burton Pasternak's article on sociology and anthropology and Fei Xiaotong's discussion at the panel. In the fall of 1981 and early in 1982, Professor Fei had the opportunity to return to the village of Kaixiangong which he had first studied in 1936. He graciously permitted Anne Thurston to translate and edit several of his reports on those visits as his contribution here. We felt that inclusion of his report, representing as it does the views of a leading Chinese social anthropologist who has been able to begin a restudy of a village where he first conducted research nearly half a century ago, would be intrinsically illuminating as well as useful in highlighting both the similarities and differences between Chinese and foreign fieldwork. While Professor Fei has approved the report included here, he has also requested that readers understand that its inclusion ought not to be read as an endorsement of the views presented by other authors.

We hope that this volume presents a case, on both academic and practical grounds, for a future expansion of fieldwork opportunities within China. Knowing that our colleagues in China will also read this volume, we have written frankly about how outsiders have coped with the opportunities so enthusiastically seized after some 30 years of isolation. In speaking frankly, we hope that our Chinese colleagues will also better understand us and that through greater understanding, some of the natural misgivings about outsiders immersing themselves deeply in Chinese society can gradually be overcome.

Finally, a note about the system of romanization employed in this volume. The texts of the articles employ the pinyin system of romanization currently in use in China, except that we have retained the conventional Western translations for the cities of Peking (Beijing in pinyin) and Canton (Guangzhou in pinyin). Many of the footnotes, however, refer to works published prior to the introduction of pinyin, and such footnotes are presented in their original spelling. Thus, for instance, the village which is romanized as Kaixiangong in pinyin often appears as Kaihsienkung in footnotes. For readers unacquainted with Western equivalencies of Chinese measures, a jin, or catty, is equal to half a kilogram or 1.1 pounds, a mu is equivalent to .067 hectares or .165 acres, and a Chinese yuan, at current rates, is $.57 U.S.

Anne F. Thurston
Burton Pasternak

Grandview, New York

Part 1

Social Science and Fieldwork in China: Context and Constraints

1. The Social Sciences and Fieldwork in China: An Overview

New Opportunities for Scholarly Exchanges with China

The autumn of 1978 represents a watershed in recent scholarly relations between the United States and the People's Republic of China. In October of that year, as relations between the two countries continued to improve (but prior to the establishment of formal diplomatic relations), China and the United States announced an agreement that would initiate substantive and long-term scholarly exchanges.

The agreement was a major and welcome departure from the exchanges that had developed in the wake of the 1972 Shanghai communique. In implementing the agreement contained in the communique to introduce and expand cultural exchanges, a number of scholarly delegations from China had visited the United States and similar numbers of American academic delegations had visited China. While these delegations had well-defined intellectual agendas and contributed to lifting the veil of misunderstanding that decades of mutual isolation had wrought, the pursuit of genuine scholarly endeavors was constrained by the mode of exchange. The visits were typically short, generally lasting from three to six weeks, thereby fostering only the type of superficial mutual understanding that the Chinese describe as "viewing flowers from horseback." The possibility that Americans and Chinese could soon begin sustained, long-term research in each others' countries represented a major departure from the earlier exchanges. The move was welcomed by the American

I am indebted to B. Michael Frolic, David Chu, and Burton Pasternak for their extensive comments on this chapter. Responsibility for its contents is solely my own.

academic community, and particularly the community of American scholars of China, with an enthusiasm that sometimes bordered on euphoria.

Exchanges in the Social Sciences

Because American scholars of China fall predominantly in the social sciences and humanities, the fires of enthusiam were further fed in the spring of 1979 with the visit to the United States of an important delegation from the national level Chinese Academy of Social Sciences (CASS). Once a branch of the Chinese Academy of Sciences, the Chinese Academy of Social Sciences had been established as a separate research organization in 1977. Headed by Huan Xiang, a distinguished Vice-President of the Academy, the delegation included among its members a number of China's best known social scientists and humanists.[1] Professor Fei Xiaotong, China's noted social anthropologist, who has contributed to this volume and who now heads the Institute of Sociology within the Academy, was a member of that delegation.

While that visit also fit the mode of "viewing flowers from horseback," its implications were nonetheless significant. Not only was this the first high-level delegation of social scientists and humanists to visit the United States in over 30 years, the visit served as a signal to the American academic community. If the Chinese would continue to give priority in scholarly exchanges to the fields of science and technology, the social sciences and humanities would nonetheless become a vital component of scholarly communication between the two countries. The social sciences and humanities in China were on the path to revitalization, and the seriousness of the projected development of the social sciences and humanities would be reflected in new opportunities for academic exchanges.[2]

---

1. In Chinese parlance, the "social sciences" include what we designate as the social sciences and the humanities. The primary focus of this presentation is the social sciences as designated in the West.

2. For a report of the visit by this delegation as well as a discussion of the national level exchange agreement, see Anne F. Thurston, "New Opportunities for Research in China," in *Items*, Volume 33, Number 2 (June 1979), pp. 15-25. For a more recent report on the status of national level agreements and negotiations, see Kenneth Prewitt, editor, *Research Opportunities in China for American Humanists and Social Scientists* (New York: Social Science Research Council, 1982).

The Structure of Exchanges

In the United States, the organization charged with implementing the flow of American scholars to China under the new national level agreement was the Committee on Scholarly Communication with the People's Republic of China (CSCPRC), the same organization that had earlier facilitated the exchange of scholarly delegations under the terms of the Shanghai communique.[3] Sponsored by the American Council of Learned Societies, the National Academy of Sciences, and the Social Science Research Council, the programs administered by the CSCPRC reflect the academic interests of its sponsoring agencies -- the humanities, natural sciences, and social sciences, respectively. Individuals supported by the CSCPRC program include both advanced graduate students and more established scholars. By early 1979, the first group of some seven American scholars had left for long-term study and research in China, and the CSCPRC has been able to send some 60 advanced graduate students and research scholars to China every academic year since the fall of 1979. The majority of these have been in the social sciences and humanities.

Following the establishment of diplomatic relations between China and the United States in January 1979, a number of universities, foundations, scholarly associations, and scientific institutions began entering into academic exchanges with counterpart organizations in China. By now, these exchanges have mushroomed to the point that it is no longer possible for merely casually interested observers to remain abreast of current exchange relations,[4] and the number of scholars going to and coming from China as part of these unofficial exchanges now far exceeds the exchanges under the nationally administered program. Moreover, in addition to formally constituted exchanges, a number of Americans have gone to China to teach in fields ranging from the natural sciences to sociology, anthropology, American literature, history and English. Some have been able to couple teaching in China with research on Chinese society. At present, some 10,000 Chinese scholars, largely in the natural sciences, engineering, and medicine, are studying and doing research at numerous academic institutions throughout

---

3. The National Committee on U.S.-China Relations was similarly charged with implementing cultural, artistic and athletic exchanges.
4. For an early assessment of the exchange relationship, see Ralph N. Clough, *A Review of the U.S.-China Exchange Program* (Washington, D.C.: Office of Research, International Communication Agency, 1981).

the United States. The number of Americans in China is
significantly smaller—several hundred at most.

This volume is about one facet of the new scholarly
exchanges with the People's Republic of China, that facet
that has to do with rural field research within China.
Indeed, the opportunity for Western historians of China to
make use of archival materials unavailable outside the
mainland is opening up new avenues of historical research and
possibilities of collaborative endeavors with Chinese
colleagues. But American scholars who take field research as
the primary mode of investigation, most notably
anthropologists and sociologists, but including political
scientists and economists as well, had especially good
reasons to welcome the new possibilities for scholarly
exchanges with China. Cut off from their natural "human
laboratory" on the mainland, these scholars had long had to
content themselves with field research on Taiwan, in Hong
Kong, or, as Martin Whyte discusses in this volume, with
interviewing refugees from the mainland who had emigrated to
Hong Kong. The possibility of conducting field research in
China under the new exchange relationship thus presented the
very exciting prospect of uniting the scholar with his
natural research milieu—the villages, factories, offices,
and urban residential areas of China.

Implementing the Exchanges

Euphoria, by its very nature, cannot be sustained, and
such has been the case as the initial enthusiasm for the new
prospects for scholarly exchanges with China have given way
to the reality of implementing those exchanges. But American
attitudes toward China have typically swung between sometimes
unquestioning adulation of that country and similarly
unrestrained pessimism. With the "opening up" of China
following President Nixon's visit in early 1972, some
American journalists who had earlier dwelled with scarcely
disguised hostility on China's shortcomings returned to the
United States to sing only China's praises.[5] As of this
writing, the pendulum has begun to swing once more from
euphoria to pessimism. Not only has the present
administration in the United States sometimes seemed less
inclined to favor China, but some of the first American
journalists to have taken up long-term residence in China in
some 30 years have now returned and published their books.

---

5. For one reporter's view of these pendulum swings, see
Stanley Karnow, "American News Media and China," in Gene T.
Hsiao, Sino-American Detente and Its Policy Implications
(New York and Washington: Praeger Publishers, 1974), pp.
76-84.

Some of what they report does not reflect with favor on China.[6]

This mood is reflected in the American academic community. The first group of American scholars to have conducted long-term research in China have now also returned. Their experiences have been remarkably diverse. Many researchers reflect with considerable satisfaction upon both the quality and depth of data they were able to gather in China and on the cooperation of their sponsoring agencies. But because opportunities to conduct research in China are still so new and the lag time between actual research and scholarly publication is so long, few reports of successful research endeavors have yet been published. Moreover, not all researchers in China have met with equal success, leading one scholar to conclude that "the dominant mood has been one of disappointment and disillusionment--a discovery that China did not achieve all that had been claimed for it in the 1970's and a realization that the Chinese social order is seriously flawed."[7] The new direction of the pendulum swing is perplexing, even exasperating, to many of our Chinese colleagues, who cannot understand why, under the oppressive rule of the "gang of four," the attitudes of Americans toward their country were so positive, while today, as China is in the process of introducing major reforms, attitudes have become so negative. Their perplexity is not entirely unwarranted.

The Moratorium on Fieldwork

But there is an additional reason for the air of caution within the academic community. Despite the successful research endeavors of many American scholars and the mutual satisfaction of both the Chinese and the American sponsoring agencies with that research, the Chinese have imposed a

6. See especially Richard Bernstein, From the Center of the Earth: The Search for the Truth about China (Boston: Little, Brown and Company, 1982), and Fox Butterfield, China: Alive in a Bitter Sea (New York: Times Books, 1982). For the similarly pessimistic account of an American teacher in China, see James Kenneson, "China Stinks." Harpers, April 1982. For less unremittingly sober accounts by Western correspondents, see David Bonavia, The Chinese (New York: Lippincott and Crowell, Publishers, 1980), and John Fraser, The Chinese: Portrait of a People (New York: Summit Books, 1980).
7. Harry Harding, "From China with Disdain: New Trends in the Study of China," Asian Survey, Volume XXII, Number 10 (October 1982), p. 936.

temporary "moratorium" on long-term fieldwork by foreigners.
Rather than being allowed to spend periods ranging from
several months to a year in the field, foreign fieldworkers
are now being permitted research stays of up to two weeks in
any given rural site, with the possibility of returning to
those sites periodically over a span of several years.

The reasons for this moratorium are undoubtedly complex.
Not only do recent tensions in Sino-American relations have
an impact on opportunities for academic exchanges, but China,
like many other countries, retains deeply ingrained
sensitivities to research by outsiders that seeks to delve
deeply into Chinese society. Moreover, because academic
fieldwork by Chinese within their own society has only
recently been revived after a hiatus of some 30 years,
potential Chinese fieldworkers are less than enthusiastic
about foreigners undertaking field research before thay have
been able to begin such research themselves. A number of
Chinese scholars have noted a certain lack of sensitivity on
the part of Western scholars toward the dilemmas faced by the
Chinese in reviving disciplines and disciplinary research
long considered taboo. And while many Chinese scholars would
prefer that fieldwork by foreigners be conducted
collaboratively with Chinese counterparts, recruiting
suitable counterparts from disciplines that have not been
practiced for 30 years has proven difficult indeed. Even
when collaboration is both possible and successful, as
Pasternak points out in his contribution to this volume, both
political and academic sensitivities remain.

However complex the factors motivating the imposition of
the moratorium may be, the reason given most publicity in the
Western press revolves around allegations that an
anthropology graduate student at Stanford University, who
conducted fieldwork in rural Guangdong on a grant from the
CSCPRC during the 1979-1980 academic year, acted contrary to
Chinese legal norms and in violation of the principles of
professional responsibility governing anthropological
research.[8] Following a lengthy investigation of these
allegations by an ad hoc review committee, the Stanford
Department of Anthropology dismissed this student from its
doctoral program.[9] Because the material contained in the

---

8. For the code of ethics governing anthropologists, see
"Statements on Ethics: Principles of Professional
Responsibility," adopted by the Council of the American
Anthropological Association (May 1971).
9. For several published reports concerning this case, see
Mike Chinoy, "American Scholar to Blame for Chinese Cutback

47 page report which led to his dismissal is said to contain material that might injure third parties, that report, as of this writing, has not been made public.

The public record contains only three incontrovertible facts: that allegations by Chinese authorities against this fieldworker began while he was still in the field and that official Chinese allegations were part of the information supplied to the Stanford investigative committee; that, following his research in China, the student published an article in a magazine on Taiwan containing accounts of forced abortions in rural Guangdong during the third trimester of pregnancy, together with unmasked photographs of Chinese women allegedly about to undergo such abortions;[10] and that the decision of dismissal has generated considerable controversy, both within the American academic community and the press.[11]   That controversy has focused on the conflict between academic freedom and the right to publish the truth on the one hand, and on the rights of human subjects on the other.   Underlying the controversy are questions about whether Stanford University in particular and scholars who have conducted (or want to conduct) research in China are compromising the integrity of academic research in order to maintain or further access to research within China—access which might be further constrained should published research findings be found offensive to the Chinese government.

The ethical issues of conducting field research in China are weighty.   But shrouded as it is in secrecy and complicated as it is by issues of private as well as scholarly ethics, this particular case is hardly the proper base from which to launch a discussion of the ethical dilemmas facing the foreign fieldworker in China. All the contributors to this volume make reference to these dilemmas,

_____

on U.S. Researchers?" Christian Science Monitor, October 6, 1981; "Trouble for a China Hand," Newsweek,, November 2, 1981; Wallace Turner, "Stanford Expels Student Faulted on China Study," Washington Post, February 26, 1983; "Battle in the Scholarly World," Time, March 14, 1983.

10. See Sunday Times China Weekly (Taiwan), May 1981.

11. See Suzanne Pepper, "Bleak Outlook for Foreign Scholars in China," Asian Wall Street Journal, March 9, 1983; "Expelling the Messenger," New York Times editorial, March 19, 1983; Frederic A. Moritz, "Scholar's dismissal raises issue of academic freedom," Christian Science Monitor, March 28, 1983; Clifford R. Barnett (Chairman, Department of Anthropology, Stanford University), New York Times letter to the editor, April 1, 1983.

and a later section of this introduction will explore those issues further.

Following the imposition of the moratorium on long-term fieldwork in early 1981, the Chinese Academy of Social Sciences began drafting a set of guidelines governing fieldwork by foreigners. While those guidelines are apparently subject to approval by both higher level state and Party agencies as well as by provincial level administrative offices, my own discussions with Chinese officials as late as April 1982 suggested that with those guidelines in place, long-term fieldwork by foreigners in China could be expected to resume. Major administrative changes within CASS were expected to slow the process of approval, and there is some indication that the draft guidelines have not met with the expected agreement from all agencies concerned. As of this writing, the publication of those guidelines, even accounting for the projected tardiness due to administrative restructuring, are several months overdue. When and if the guidelines are forthcoming, it is entirely possible that foreign fieldworkers will be confronted with a new set of ethical dilemmas with respect to fieldwork in China—with the question of whether the constraints they may impose are or are not outweighed by what one can learn.

Steven Butler opens his contribution to this volume by declaring that "successful fieldwork in China is possible." Both his contribution and the pieces by other contributors attest to that fact. But it must be noted that the Americans who report here on their fieldwork were in China during the high point of Sino-American relations and the period of greatest liberalization within China since the establishment of the People's Republic. The constraints under which they labored are not only not likely to be eased, they are likely to become institutionalized. Moreover, it is possible, even likely, that those constraints will be tightened.

In the meantime, both the current moratorium on long-term fieldwork and the recent revival within the U.S. of questions relating to the ethical responsibilities of foreign fieldworkers offer us the opportunity to stop and take stock of the possibilities and potential pitfalls of fieldwork in China. In focusing on fieldwork in China, this volume is designed to accomplish several tasks: first, to examine the current state of and future prospects for the development of sociology and anthropology in China and to link the state of those disciplines to the possibility for fieldwork by "outsiders" there; second, to offer a number of perspectives on the experiences of field researchers in China and to compare the intellectual "payoffs" of research in China with research at its gate, in Hong Kong; and finally, to broach the question of what has been learned from research within China and whether the value of what scholars can learn outweighs the constraints within which they must operate.

Both the views presented in this volume and the means by which the contributors obtained permission to undertake their research are diverse. My own research in China, supported by the National Endowment for the Humanities, was a study of the "victims" of China's Cultural Revolution and combined a study of the so-called "literature of the wounded" about the Cultural Revolution with extensive interviews of victims of that period. Background for the overview provided here comes from my experience as former staff to the China programs at the Social Science Research Council, as staff to a delegation to China of scholars representing the China committees of the Social Science Research Council[12] and the American Council of Learned Societies in 1979-1980, and through nine months (1981-1982) of research in China, affiliated with both Peking Normal University and with the Institute of Literature of the Chinese Academy of Social Sciences.

Burton Pasternak, who provides an overview of the current status of sociology and anthropology in China and who offers some very concrete advice to scholars contemplating field research there, was co-chair of the 1979-1980 delegation of China specialists and has had considerable experience conducting fieldwork on rural Taiwan. In 1981-82, he conducted six months of fieldwork—a social demographic study of an urban neighborhood—in Tianjin city. A collaborative project with two Chinese colleagues, his research was supported by the CSCPRC and the National Science Foundation.

Martin Whyte has not actually done fieldwork in the People's Republic of China, but his work on contemporary Chinese society is known to anyone with more than a casual interest in that country.[13] He and his colleague William Parish, from the University of Chicago, have pioneered a sophisticated methodology for studying China from a distance.

---

12. For a report of this delegation, including descriptions of the current status of the separate social science and humanities disciplines, see Anne F. Thurston and Jason H. Parker, editors, Humanistic and Social Science Research in China: Recent History and Future Prospects (New York: Social Science Research Council, 1980).
13. See, in particular, William L. Parish and Martin King Whyte, Village and Family in Contemporary China (Chicago: The University of Chicago Press, 1978).

The insights Whyte offers on the comparative value of research in China and research at its gate are particularly timely in light of the current diminution of fieldwork opportunities in China.

In reporting here on his recent visits to the village of Kaixiangong, Fei Xiaotong presents the views of one of China's most noted social anthropologists on recent changes in the Chinese countryside as reflected in the village he first studied in 1936. Through a projected series of visits to Kaixiangong over the next several years, Fei hopes eventually to provide an update to his classic book, Peasant Life in China, first published in 1939.[14] Kaixiangong has recently been designated a "field research station," and new Chinese graduate students in sociology will have an opportunity to conduct field research in that village and its surrounding region.

Helen Siu, an anthropologist trained at Stanford University, is a Hong Kong Chinese who is currently resident in the United States where she is on the faculty at Yale University. Her experience conducting a series of field visits to rural Guangdong over a period of several years should have applicability to other scholars operating within the framework currently governing fieldwork in China-- short-term visits over extended periods of time. Her contribution combines a theory of cyclical policy change with actual observation of how those policy changes have affected local industrial development in one commune.

Norma Diamond was able to conduct field research in Taitou village by combining a year of teaching at Shandong University with several months of research, another mode which may become increasingly possible to foreign field researchers. While anthropologists frequently point to the potential value of restudying rural communities, Diamond, like Fei, is unusual in actually having done so. Her work represents a restudy of a village first written about in 1945 by anthropologist Martin Yang,[15] himself a native of the village.

The research of Steven Butler, a political scientist, was sponsored by the CSCPRC and was implemented under the auspices of the Chinese Academy of Social Sciences. Butler's experience is unique in that he was actually able to live in

14. Hsiao-tung Fei, Peasant Life in China (London: Routledge and Kegan Paul, 1939).
15. Martin C. Yang, A Chinese Village: Taitou, Shantung Province (New York: Columbia University Press, 1945).

the community he was studying. Focusing on the impact of rural economic development on local administration, Butler's advice to other scholars about how to conduct successful field research in China is both concrete and upbeat.

The variety of means through which the scholars who contributed to this volume gained access to China suggests no single pattern. In the future, the routes to fieldwork in China are likely to become even more diverse. For most American scholars without personal ties to individuals or academic institutions in China, the most probable route to field research for the foreseeable future is through the national exchanges sponsored by the CSCPRC. As the agency designated by the American government to facilitate the flow of American scholars to China, the CSCPRC is both a funding and negotiating agency and is actively involved in the placement of those scholars it selects for study and research. As the agency officially charged with implementing exchanges, however, the capacity of the CSCPRC to place scholars in the field remains more sensitive to fluctuations in Sino-American relations. When Sino-American relations are relatively smooth, the CSCPRC can be expected successfully to exert considerable leverage in its placement of scholars. But that leverage can be expected to decline during periods of tension. With the increasing plurality of exchanges between Chinese and American academic institutions and the expanded channels of communication afforded through these unofficial exchanges, alternative routes of access may be increasingly available, as the experiences of Diamond and Siu, reported in this volume, attest. Other scholars have conducted short-term field research through arrangements worked out directly with the Chinese Ministry of Education or through university-to-university exchanges. Thus, it is possible that in the long run, the more stable pattern of exchanges may be through university-to-university or other individual, unofficial agreements where fluctuations in Sino-American relations are less likely to have a major effect. To the extent this volume offers advice to future field researchers in China, that advice is premised less on how to obtain permission to conduct field research than on how to proceed when and if that permission has been granted.

Fieldwork in China will remain, for most Americans, a challenging, occasionally harrowing, but potentially rewarding experience. We hope that the variety of viewpoints presented in this volume will serve to modulate the current swing of the pendulum, that the overall message is sober without being pessimistic, realistic without being discouraging. It is our hope that the experiences of those who have already conducted fieldwork can serve to prepare others who may follow them to the field, rendering the path that others may tread later a little bit smoother.

Field research, by its very nature, is more sensitive than other forms of research. Scientists who investigate physical causation can perhaps most easily bridge the political and cultural differences that sometimes impede scholarly communication in other academic disciplines. While the fruits of historical research may sometimes challenge strongly felt indigenous beliefs, historians nonetheless work primarily with documents. It is in social science field research where the subject of investigation is human beings in the here and now that the possibilities for misunderstandings due to divergent scholarly traditions, differences in politics and culture, and different conceptions both about the rights of the subjects under investigation and of the obligations of the researcher, stand the greatest chance of becoming magnified. Based on their experiences in China or at its gate, the contributors to this volume address problems they faced in the field. In this introductory section, I would like to address these questions in a more general way and also to raise the more substantive question of the value to the social sciences of fieldwork in China.

Divergent Scholarly Traditions

The Scholar and the State

At the heart of the difference between Chinese and Western conceptions of the role of the scholar and the function of scholarship is the relation of the scholarly enterprise to the state. Both in traditional Chinese society and today, the scholar has functioned in service to the state. The route to academic success in traditional China was through sufficient mastery of the Confucian classics to pass the imperial civil service exams. Success in those exams provided entry into the elite class of scholar-bureaucrats whose function was to administer the complex national bureaucracy. Academics and politics in China have long been linked.

But the role of the scholar-bureaucrat was not without its tensions, and instances of conflict between the individual conscience of the Confucian scholar and the role he was asked to play by the state contribute much to traditional lore. While the Taoist tradition once permitted scholars who disagreed with the throne to withdraw from active public service, those who stood by their consciences to challenge the throne were also aware that the result of that challenge might be punishment, exile, or even death.

The social sciences were introduced to and began to develop in China on the heels of imperial collapse, during the country's period of greatest revolutionary upheaval and prior to the re-establishment, in 1949, of a viable political state. The first generation of Chinese social scientists were not servants of the state, but they did consider themselves servants of the nation—social reformers in search of solutions to the country's pressing social, political, and economic problems. The social sciences were embraced by Chinese intellectuals, to some extent at least, in the belief that the social sciences could contribute to the solution of those problems. While the lot of China's early[16] social scientists was an exceptionally difficult one, they nonetheless engaged in unprecedented freedom of debate. That situation was to change with the re-establishment of political order. China's socialist state has not always treated its social scientists well.

The Decline of the Social Sciences

Beginning in 1952, when China began reorganizing its universities in emulation of the Soviet model, a number of social science disciplines, sociology and political science among them, were disbanded, their previous practitioners being dispersed to other departments or compelled to begin completely different academic or other pursuits. Anthropology, to the extent it survived, was practiced largely in academies or institutes of national minorities studies.

During the brief blossoming of the so-called Hundred Flowers campaign of 1956 and 1957, when Chinese intellectuals were encouraged to offer criticisms of Communist Party policy, a number of social scientists cautiously suggested that the social sciences did have a legitimate role to play in a socialist society. Qian Duansheng, a distinguished, Harvard-trained political scientist, served as spokesman for the restoration of political science. Several sociologists trained prior to 1949 formed a "work preparatory committee on sociology" and wrote in favor of the reintroduction of sociology into China. Fei Xiaotong was a member of that

---

16. For one description of the wartime lot of some such scholars, see John King Fairbank, Chinabound (New York: Harper and Row, Publishers, Inc., 1982), particularly pp. 223-240.

group and both spoke in favor of the reintroduction of sociology and made his second field trip to the village of Kaixiangong.[17] Most who spoke in favor of the revival of the social sciences were branded as "rightists" during the movement that brought the Hundred Flowers campaign to a decisive halt.

The impact of the Cultural Revolution (1966-1976) on China's intellectual community and on individual Chinese scholars has become, in its broad outlines at least, only too painfully clear. Universities, for periods of time ranging from two to seven or eight years, were closed, and many of them reopened to serve "worker, peasant, soldier" students, many of whom were ill-prepared for higher education. University curricula consequently were also diluted, reflecting both the academic limitations of the new students, the political view that courses should be guided by the "thought of Mao Zedong," and the demand that educational content be directly linked to immediate, practical goals.

Most libraries throughout China were closed for a substantial part of the Cultural Revolution, and on many campuses, large numbers of books, particularly those by foreign authors, were burned. In some cases, libraries were ransacked and card catalogues destroyed. Replacing those books and restoring order to China's libraries now requires substantial capital investment as well as trained library personnel. The needs in both regards exceed China's current capacities.

---

17. Other members of the preparatory committee included Wu Jingchao (now deceased), who was the first publicly to raise the issue of revival in January 1957; Li Jinghan, now an advisor to the Chinese Sociological Association; Lei Jieqiong, currently a vice-mayor of Peking; Chen Da (deceased); and Yuan Fang, currently chairman of the Sociology Department at Peking University. For a further discussion of the efforts to revive sociology in 1957, see David Chu, "The Non-Development and Development of Chinese Sociology after 1949," Ph.D dissertation, in progress, University of California, Berkeley. I am grateful to David Chu for pointing out the existence and activities of this group. For the statements made by Fei Xiaotong at the time, see Fei Hsiao-t'ung, "A Few Words on Sociology," and "A Revisit to Kaihsienkung," in James P. McGough, editor and translator, *Fei Hsiao-t'ung: The Dilemma of a Chinese Intellectual* (White Plains, N.Y.: M.E. Sharpe, Inc. 1979), pp. 32-75.

Individual intellectuals and intellectuals as a class came under sustained and often vicious attack during the Cultural Revolution. Many who had been educated or had family members abroad, particularly those with ties to the United States, were accused of being spies. Many intellectuals were incarcerated during this period, and most, whether directly attacked or not, were sent to so-called "May 7th Cadre Schools" to participate in agricultural labor and receive "political re-education."

The Revival of the Social Sciences

Both the social sciences and individual social scientists began to be "rehabilitated" under the more pragmatic policies introduced by Deng Xiaoping following the downfall of the "gang of four" in 1976, and both the boldness with which Deng has reversed earlier "leftist" excesses and the renewed commitment to the development of the social sciences have since continued without major reversals. But the path along which the social sciences have been revived has not always been a smooth one, and to equate restoration with a vindication of the social sciences as practiced in the 1930's and 1940's would be a mistake. While social scientists are being asked to function once more in the role of social reformers, they are also asked to perform that role in service to the state. Moreover, unlike the scholar-bureaucrat of an earlier era, while social scientists in contemporary China are closely tied and have access to the state bureaucracy, they nonetheless stand outside it. They are encouraged to offer advice on policy considerations, but they are not part of the decision-making apparatus. And the status of the contemporary Chinese scholar within his own society is considerably less prestigious or influential than that of the scholar-bureaucrat—a diminution of status given particular impetus by the Cultural Revolution but also fostered through several decades of official suspicion of intellectuals. Together with the revival of the social sciences is an attempt to enhance the status of Chinese intellectuals, both by recognizing the indispensible role they must play in current plans for the modernization of China and by attempting to offer them financial compensation commensurate with their newly assigned role.

But however much the official ideology may have changed in the years following the death of Mao in 1976, state ideology does serve to direct, channel, and constrain the development of contemporary Chinese social science. Two of these constraints, in particular, should be noted.

Constraints on the Revival of the Social Sciences

First, at the most general level, the direction of research in China today is dictated by and phrased in terms of service to the goals of the "four modernizations."[18] Moreover, after a brief period of unprecedented academic debate in 1978-1979, the national level leadership set forth four "basic principles" governing the limits within which academic debate in China can take place. Scholars must indicate adherence to Marxism-Leninism-Mao Zedong thought; commitment to socialism; acceptance of the dictatorship of the proletariat; and acceptance of the leadership of the Chinese Communist Party.

In practice, the relationship between the official guidelines and particular research is sometimes obscure, and even within the constraints under which Chinese intellectuals labor, there is considerable leeway for lively discussion, disagreement, and debate. Chinese scholars and administrators at all levels recognize that their country is going through a period of transition, a period where many answers have yet to be found. Indeed, every foreign academic in China will meet "scholars" and administrators who reflect the pages of the People's Daily so accurately that those foreigners who feel compelled to read that newspaper could have written the monologues themselves. But foreigners can expect to meet a greater number of people who reflect genuine, well-informed, and intelligent concern about their country's development, good humor about some of their countrymen's foibles, and complaints about many aspects of their daily lives.

Nonetheless, the political basis of the current revival of the social sciences suggests fundamental differences between Chinese and Westerners over the very meaning of "the social sciences." While the Western academic tradition permits considerable cross-over between government and academics, Western scholars are nonetheless free to pursue "scholarship for scholarship's sake." The fact that scholarship in China will be harnessed to the goals of a modernizing, socialist state raises the question of whether, in a Marxist-Leninist state, the development of an autonomous social science is possible.

Secondly, the different bases of the social sciences in China and the West have an effect on the extent to which the Chinese social sciences can be expected to become integrated

18. The "four modernizations" are in agriculture, industry, science and technology, and the military.

into internationally coordinated research endeavors. At a time when many Western social scientists are beginning to consider seriously the goal of "internationalizing" the social sciences, the Chinese goal is articulated in terms of the development of an indigenous, distinctively Chinese, and more specifically, Chinese Marxist, social science. While the Chinese recognize that with the 30 year hiatus of social science training and research, the goal of modernizing their social sciences can be speeded through the study of Western social science, they remain wary of being overly influenced by the West. This wariness can be seen as the contemporary socialist equivalent of the traditional ti-yong distinction, best captured in the old slogan, "Chinese learning for essence, Western learning for practice." At root, the persistence of the ti-yong distinction seems to be based on a fear that in the process of modernizing, China runs the risk of losing something quintessentially Chinese, something fundamental to Chinese national identity. Accordingly, in studying Western social science, the Chinese will attempt to separate the "essence" of Western social science (its underlying philosophies and theories) from what is modern and "practical" (its research techniques), substituting Chinese for Western essence.

This is not to suggest that there are not important points of convergence between Chinese and Western social science. Alongside the official guidelines that serve to channel the development of Chinese social science stands the dictum to "seek truth from facts," a dictum that has resulted in a renewed emphasis on the necessity of "social investigation" (shehui diaocha) by China's social scientists. Simple and obvious though this slogan may appear to Western scholars, it represents a considerable departure from the Cultural Revolution era when truth and fact were frequently twisted, distorted, or ignored in the service of political ideology. The new opportunity to seek truth from facts—to conduct empirical research—is welcome indeed to many members of the Chinese academic community.

Moreover, the guidelines governing academic research articulated at the national level are not always so faithfully heeded by the individual scholar. The mere fact that academic salaries are paid by the state and alternative sources of income are difficult to obtain has rendered obsolete the Taoist tradition of withdrawal to a solitary and contemplative life. But residues of the tradition persist. Some scholars, content quietly to pursue their academic pursuits without particular official recognition, are able to remain remarkably aloof from official political concerns.

Continuing Tensions within the Social Sciences in China

The role assigned to the contemporary Chinese social scientist, even more than the role of the traditional scholar-bureaucrat, remains fraught with tensions. To be sure, many -- probably most -- Chinese intellectuals are comfortable in their roles as social reformers, and the goal of modernization, however amorphous that goal may be, seems universally shared. But China's social scientists remain vulnerable to attack at several levels.

Both the closest and highest-level link between the state and the social scientist is within the Chinese Academy of Social Sciences. As China embarks on a series of economic, political, social, and legal reforms that would have been unthinkable, and branded as "capitalistic," during the militant radicalism of the Cultural Revolution, some scholars at the Chinese Academy of Social Sciences are being called upon to provide intellectual guidance and the legitimating rationale for a host of new policies.[19] The conceptual difficulties of articulating an ideology that supports socialism during a period when the meaning of socialism in China is in considerable doubt, and that adheres to the thought of Mao while Mao's "mistakes" are under public criticism, are taxing indeed. Should the intellectuals within the Academy fail to fulfill the role assigned to them, both social science and social scientists could suffer.

On the other hand, while the state of Chinese academic institutions is still evolving, there is some indication that the Academy of Social Sciences is being granted a greater measure of intellectual autonomy than initially presumed, that it may evolve more in the direction of an academic research academy than a government "think tank." In a few instances where the Chinese government has faced a choice between locating such "think tanks" within the Academy or directly under the State Council, the State Council has formed research groups directly under its sponsorship, outside the Academy, thereby preserving a measure of intellectual autonomy for the Academy.

The link between CASS and the national level state bureaucracy is mirrored within both provincial level academies of social science and Chinese universities.

---

19. For an interesting argument that this is essentially the function of the social scientist in the Western world, see Francis X. Sutton, "Rationality, Development, and Scholarship," *Items*, Volume 36, Number 4 (December 1982), p. 50.

Research plans within provincial level social science
academies are often closely linked to practical policy
questions as perceived by provincial level authorities, and
research within universities is often directed toward the
city or province in which they are located. Nonetheless,
universities, impressionistically at least, seem to function
with somewhat greater autonomy than either the national or
provincial level social science research academies.

Moreover, fears of many Western scholars concerning the
potential vulnerability of Chinese social scientists
investigating the practical implications of official Party
policies have yet to materialize. These fears have usually
been expressed in terms of the possible implications for
individual scholars and the development of the social
sciences if research were to suggest alternatives at odds
with prevailing political policies. In fact, investigations
by Chinese social scientists have revealed a number of
unintended consequences of official policies, and these
unintended consequences are thus far being discussed with a
frankness inconceivable only a few years ago. The
consequences for China's birth control policies of a rural
responsibility system which places a premium on labor, for
instance, are being openly discussed, and an increase in the
rate of female infanticide has been publicly admitted.[20]
Indeed, the legacy of both the anti-rightist campaign of 1957
and of the Cultural Revolution may serve to impede scholars
from proposing alternatives greatly at odds with prevailing
policy, but the current direction is still toward greater
openness and frankness.

Finally, there is the question of how Chinese can borrow
Western social science techniques while remaining confident
that they are nonetheless building an indigenous,
distinctively Chinese, and Marxist, social science. The
attempts to separate form from essence in the past have not
often been regarded as successful, and the recent opening to
the West in China has been accompanied by apparently
increasing fears of "Westernization." Chinese scholars
currently studying Western social science are being asked to
walk a very fine line. To cross that line is to risk
criticism, and if such criticism were to become strong
enough, not only could individual scholars suffer but the
very real progress in scholarly communication between Western
and Chinese social scientists could be jeopardized. Moreover,
China's insistence upon the development of an indigenous

---

20. See, for instance, "Protecting Infant Girls," Beijing
Review, Volume 26, Number 5 (January 31, 1983), p. 4.

social science and its continuing preoccupation with possible adverse consequences of Western influence has a very real effect on possibilities for collaborative research between Chinese and Western social scientists, as Pasternak details in the following chapter.

This brief review of China's different conceptions of the role and function of scholarship leads to two, not entirely compatible, conclusions. First, despite the fragile base upon which the social sciences began their hesitant revival in 1977 and the continued vulnerability of the social sciences to any major political change in China, that base has now been substantially strengthened, and the legitimacy of developing the social sciences in the service of Chinese socialism remains, if not unchallenged, at least relatively secure. Secondly, whatever the end product of China's goal of developing its social sciences may be, Chinese social science will differ substantially from ours. To be sure, there will be many points of convergence, not the least of which is China's renewed commitment to empirical research. And there will be many topics of common interest and many shared research techniques. Pasternak's discussion of current trends in anthropology and sociology details both those points of convergence and the difficulties engendered by differing research goals, techniques, and bureaucratic practices. If the gaps that divide Western and Chinese social science can not always be closed, they can sometimes be bridged.

Differences in Politics and Culture

There is a Chinese saying, more or less equivalent to "when in Rome, do as the Romans," that roughly translates, "when going to a foreign country, it is best first to inquire into its customs." Many foreigners undertaking research in China will already know a great deal about Chinese customs, and some will already have lived in Chinese communities, usually in Hong Kong or Taiwan, outside the mainland. A number of Chinese customs will bear directly on the research experience.

The foreign researcher in China will inevitably be categorized as a "foreign guest," a label that carries with it a set of contradictory implications. As Butler points out, cooperation will be considerably enhanced if one comes also to be viewed as a "friend." But these are labels applied by and operative within the academic unit with which the foreign researcher is affiliated. The foreign researcher in China, very much in contrast to the tourist, will also come into contact with a wide variety of Chinese with widely different responsibilities in the Chinese social system, who will also hold widely divergent views of the foreign researcher.

Among the various types of Chinese one can expect to meet are other intellectuals, the staff of the academic institution sponsoring one's research, the Public Security Bureau, service personnel in a variety of capacities, taxi drivers, the local officials at one's field site, and ordinary Chinese. While the objective of some of these people may be to make the researcher's stay as fruitful and productive as possible, the objective of others sometimes seems to be to make it uncomfortable, if not downright impossible. While some will treat the foreign researcher with elaborate courtesy, others will be disconcertingly indifferent or even rude. Some will suggest that you stay forever, while others may give barely disguised indication that they wish you would go away. If those who seem to wish you would go away are also in any way involved in implementing one's project, the foreign researcher has suffered a stroke of bad luck representing a potentially insurmountable obstacle to the project's successful execution.

On Being a Foreigner in China

The Chinese have a well-developed sense of insider and outsider, both within their own society and between Chinese and foreigners. Chinese from Peking continue to insist that Cantonese will eat anything, and people from Shanghai unabashedly proclaim the superiority of their native place. To listen to young people tell about their far-flung travels during the "revolutionary linkups" _qua_ sightseeing excursions during the Cultural Revolution is to encounter anew the regional stereotypes through which Chinese have long described each other. But there seems to be general agreement that despite the differences that distinguish Chinese from one another, foreigners are more different still. What is more, some branches of Chinese officialdom continue to regard foreigners—and their potential influence—with a considerable degree of suspicion. Just as it was the custom in imperial China to isolate foreign missionaries and traders from easy contact with Chinese, so informal contacts between Chinese and foreigners today continue to be discouraged.

Anti-foreign (and anti-American) attitudes persist at all levels of Chinese society, and it is the task of some, most notably representatives of the Public Security Bureau, to monitor—indeed, to discourage—contacts between Chinese and foreigners. A Chinese from one work unit visiting another is routinely asked to register at a service desk. Chinese visiting foreigners in their hotels or dormitories are similarly asked to register, and such visits may well be reported to the work unit of the visitor. Explanations for such procedures range from the reasonable to the absurd, and include the necessity to protect the foreigners from "bad" Chinese, such as common thieves; from young women seeking foreign husbands; or from young students looking for a "back door" to study abroad. Chinese similarly have been warned that among the ranks of foreigners are those who are "spies", and the Chinese definition of "spy" is rather different from ours. Activities that might be considered quite appropriate for a foreign researcher in China may be regarded as a "theft of state secrets" by a foreigner whose official function in China is to teach.

At the heart of the difference between the Chinese and American conception of "spy" may be the elaborate set of categories attached to various foreigners temporarily resident in China. Whether the foreigner is labelled a tourist, a foreign expert (a teacher), an undergraduate or graduate student, or a foreign scholar will have considerable bearing on what the foreigner is permitted to do. A tourist, after all, is expected to sightsee, a foreign expert to teach, a student to study, and a foreign scholar to conduct research. For a foreign expert to attempt to conduct research without official permission is to risk serious misunderstanding and potential jeopardy to Chinese friends who may have assisted in that research.[21] Given the strong constraints placed on contact between Chinese and foreigners and the suspicion with which foreigners continue to be viewed, field research by an outsider is impossible without the support and cooperation of officialdom, as all the contributors to this volume make clear and Pasternak and Butler describe in considerable detail.

Nonetheless, many Chinese are genuinely desirous of establishing friendships with foreigners, and some are

---

21. For reports of how far such misunderstandings have gone in one case, see Michael Weisskopf, "China Holds American as Suspect in Spy Case," and "China Reported Set to Expel American Held in Spy Case," Washington Post, June 2 & 3, 1982; and "U.S. Teacher Ordered to Leave China," Beijing Review, June 14, 1982, p. 7. For the possibly larger political dimensions of this case, see "Protesting U.S. Checking of Chinese Diplomats Luggage," Beijing Review, May 24, 1982, p.7; and Fox Butterfield, "Testing the Limits of U.S.-China Exchanges," New York Times, April 8, 1982, p. 20E.

able to do so with only minimal constraints. Many leading
intellectuals have been officially "cleared" for contact with
foreigners and can maintain those contacts with little fear
of immediate reprisal. In other cases, intellectuals will
request permission from their work unit before agreeing to a
meeting or even ask that the meeting be arranged under
official, and therefore officially sanctioned, auspices.
Some Chinese have full time jobs dealing with foreigners, and
long-term associations often blossom into friendships.
Others feel free to pursue contacts with foreigners because
the leader of their work unit does not object. Many
contacts, of course, can be carried out only with utmost
discretion.

The living arrangements the foreign researcher is able
to make in China are likely to have a major bearing on the
extent of informal contact he is able to have with Chinese.
The forthcoming regulations governing fieldwork are likely to
discourage researchers from actually living among their
respondents. Urban-based researchers should consider the
possibility of living in a campus dormitory or a small guest
house open to both Chinese and foreigners in lieu of an
exclusively foreign hotel. While such accommodations may not
place some researchers in any closer contact with their
respondents, they do render informal contact easier.
Personnel charged with signing in visitors at such places
often like their jobs little more than we, and registration
procedures are often lax.

On Being a "Guest"

However diverse the reactions of the variety of Chinese
with whom the foreigner comes into contact may be, within the
academic unit with which he is affiliated, the researcher
will be viewed as a "guest." The constraints of being a
foreigner are both mitigated and enhanced by also being a
guest—mitigated because guests are treated with genuine
courtesy and enhanced because the courtesies accorded the
guest can also serve to impede contact.

Few cultures treat their guests with more lavish
courtesy than the Chinese. To be a guest is to be special,
and to be special is to be accorded privileges of housing,
food, and transportation far above what is ordinary to most
Chinese. Moreover, no matter how long one's research stay or
how uncomfortable the role may sometimes prove to be, most
foreign researchers in China find it difficult to escape the
elaborate rituals associated with being a guest. As Butler

points out, escape is all the more difficult in the fishbowl existence of the field researcher who is actually able to live in the field. But as Butler also points out, all sides recognize the ritualistic qualities of the roles of host and guest. The trick, for the foreign researcher, is not just to learn the etiquette but to play the role well.

The elaborate courtesies accorded a "foreign guest" are not unique to socialist China, nor are they confined to Chinese on the mainland. Being the guest of a Chinese anywhere is likely to involve an elaborate etiquette that contrasts sharply with the greater informality of the West. The Chinese host can be expected to put his very best foot forward, all the while denying it. For the guest to be other than gracious and grateful, according to Chinese custom, would be rude.

Nonetheless, some foreigners come to consider the elaborate courtesies Chinese accord their guests excessive, and this is all the more true for researchers determined to overcome the substantial barriers that stand between them and ordinary Chinese. The role of guest can serve to separate the foreign scholar from the very people he has come to study and to understand.

On Becoming a "Friend"

As Butler and Siu point out, much of the wariness toward the foreign guest may be moderated in time if the guest comes to be regarded as a "friend." And with the evolution of foreign researcher from guest to friend can come a heightened level of cooperation between the researcher and his hosts. Successful research may be possible if the researcher does not come to be viewed as a friend, but is considerably easier if he is.

What this suggests is that the human element—intangible factors of personality, adaptability, geniality, sensitivity, and decorum—play a far greater role in the success of research in China than many Westerners are either accustomed to or might consider appropriate. The foreign researcher will be judged not just by his merit as a scholar but also by his personal qualities. Here is another instance of substantial difference between Chinese and American academic norms.

In contrast to an earlier period of recent history, however, the "friend" is not expected to be a sycophant. Aside from important but more indefinable qualities of graciousness, good humor, and flexibility, two factors seem most important in determining whether the foreigner will come to be regarded as a friend. The first is whether one's Chinese hosts believe that the researcher, upon his departure, will give an "objective" account of his experiences--both personal and scholarly--while there. There is a political component to the Chinese conception of objectivity. While the Chinese do not expect uncritical acceptance of their socialist system, and sometimes invite criticisms of particular shortcomings, they would hope that criticisms be balanced by a recognition of the achievements and accomplishments of the past 30 years. Researchers with a blanket hostility toward a socialist system, whose frustrations at the impediments to achieving their research goals are expressed in terms of resentment, or who are working on topics or in research sites where accomplishments of the past three decades are difficult to discern, will confront a greater number of barriers to their attempts to elicit cooperation.

A second factor contributing to the recognition of the foreign researcher as "friend" is trust, which can be built up only after the foreign researcher has had time to demonstrate that he can be trusted. Foreigners coming to China after having established good relations with particular individuals or academic institutions in China can reduce or eliminate the time it takes to build that trust, but for others, patience is required until it develops. The research that I conducted in China, for instance, was not fieldwork, but it did involve many interviews, the majority of which I was able to conduct in private, and was on an exceptionally sensitive topic--the victims of China's Cultural Revolution. At the conclusion of my research, I asked some of my hosts at the Chinese Academy of Social Sciences why they had permitted me to carry out this sensitive project. The answer was that they trusted me and believed that I was a friend of the Chinese people. Because my relations with the Chinese with whom I was most closely associated were genuinely warm and cordial, and because of my great satisfaction at having accomplished my research goals, I feel quite comfortable with the perception of me as a "friend." In fact, I would be extremely disappointed had the perception been otherwise, because I also regard those with whom I was closely associated very much as friends.

But many foreign researchers may remain uncomfortable with the knowledge that the success of their research depends to some extent on becoming a friend. The goal of most foreign researchers is less, as the Chinese phrase it, "to promote the friendship between the Chinese and American people," than to advance our social scientific understanding of Chinese society. Others will feel frustrated if the mix of personality, interest, and competence between the foreign researcher and the person or persons assigned to work with him are simply not conducive to cooperative interaction. The dilemma for the foreign researcher is that the success of his project is fundamentally dependent on cooperation, which is, in some measure, contingent upon his being regarded as a "friend."

The Rights of Subjects and
the Obligations of the Researcher

Perhaps the most difficult problem the foreign researcher will face, both in the field and upon return, are dilemmas of scholarly ethics. Field researchers in China can expect to confront ethical dilemmas relating to issues of confidentiality and rights of subjects on the one hand and to possibly divergent expectations of and obligations to Chinese and Western audiences on the other.

Confidentiality and the Rights of Subjects

As Diamond and Whyte point out in their contributions to this volume, protection of the rights of subjects is a fundamental tenet of the ethics of American scholarship, and the guarantee of respondents' anonymity is fundamental to that protection. Scholarly associations in the United States have drawn up codes of ethics for the disciplines they represent, and federal funding of research is contingent upon the scholar's ability to demonstrate that he will, in conducting and publishing his research, be able to protect the rights of those individuals who are the subject of his research.

Because field research in China can only be conducted with the cooperation and assistance of officials at several levels of the state bureaucracy, and because interviews with respondents are rarely completely private, it is often impossible to protect the anonymity of subjects from those in China charged with implementing the foreigner's field research. While the problem may be minimal when the foreign researcher is simply trying to collect a statistical sample on a relatively apolitical topic, the problem is considerably heightened in ethnographic and other research where the texture and complexity of Chinese life and revelation of anecdotal material are important. The orthodoxy, or at least acceptability, of today may become the heresy of tomorrow, and Chinese citizens still stand unprotected against the possibility of charges in the future for revelations that were acceptable in the past. Nor is there anything the foreigner can do to protect them against possible reprisal.

In his evaluation of the relative merits of research in Hong Kong versus fieldwork in China, Martin Whyte deals quite explicitly with the moral questions facing the field researcher in China. While he refuses, in the balance sheet with which he concludes his discussion, to view research in China versus research in Hong Kong in the context of "either/or," when the confidentiality of interviews remains of primary consideration for the scholar, Whyte argues, Hong Kong is unquestionably the preferred research site. That this severely limits the nature and range of research projects that can be undertaken in China, there can be no doubt. Indeed, Whyte suggests that for researchers with sufficient time and resources, a research strategy that combines interviewing in Hong Kong with research in China is likely to prove most fruitful. The articles by Siu and Butler support his contention. Other scholars have used research in China to provide a statistical base, relying on interviews in Hong Kong to provide supplementary anecdotal material.

Divergent Audiences

A second problem concerns the divergent audiences to whom the foreign field researcher's work is addressed. The foreign researcher who arrives in China believing that he is gathering material for research that will ultimately be addressed to a Western audience soon learns that there will be at least two audiences for his research, one Western and one Chinese. The expectations and sensibilities of these two audiences may be divergent. For instance, in the course of his research, the foreigner is likely to come across material, whether in written form or through observation and conversation, that the Chinese will regard as neibu, as "internal," information that the Chinese will not want reported abroad. The neibu category remains perplexing to many foreigners, ranging as it does from unpublished drafts of scholarly research to information that would similarly be considered classified in the United States. In justifying the recent imprisonment of a Chinese reporter for revealing "state secrets" to foreigners, the official Chinese press declared that, "before they are made public, all of the Party's private activities are state secrets."[22] Neibu information to which the foreign fieldworker may be exposed may be related to problems remaining unsolved or to problems being solved through means that Westerners might consider

---

22. "Crime of Betraying State Secrets," *Beijing Review*, May 17, 1982, p. 3.

unacceptable. It may concern disagreements and hostilities between a local populace and its leadership or between leadership groups at different levels of the hierarchy. Economic reports that suggest that policies are not producing the desired effect, or reports on areas that have not greatly advanced under socialism may also be considered neibu, as may information on personal behavior that violates official norms. Does the foreigner report such information or not? And if so, how does he protect those who have provided him with such information against possible future reprisals?

Fieldwork in China is still too new to provide clear-cut answers to these questions. Few reports from the field have been published. Academic sponsors in China recognize that the continued credibility of the foreign scholar depends on thorough and accurate reporting. How the fieldworker reports sensitive information will influence China's attitude toward that report. There is no doubt that the use of sensitive materials for political rather than academic purposes will be greeted with considerable consternation both in China and the West. But the limits to accurate and thorough reporting--whether scholars who incorporate sensitive material into their published academic studies will continue to be welcomed in China--has yet to be tested. More discussion of these troublesome issues within the Western academic community is needed.

This presentation has thus far focused largely on the constraints the foreign fieldworker will face in China--on the compromises and accommodations that may be necessary in order to conduct successful fieldwork. A final question remains. What, given the limitations that are likely to continue, are the potential intellectual payoffs to field research in China?

The Intellectual Payoffs to Field Research in China

The scholars who report substantively on their fieldwork in this volume all conducted research in rural China. With the exception of the selection by Helen Siu, all the contributions were written very shortly after return from the field, before the researcher had had time fully to analyze his or her data. The substantive reports contained in this volume must therefore be considered preliminary. Moreover, because these contributions are based on presentations made at a panel at the annual meeting of the American Association for the Advancement of Science, the contributors did not have the opportunity for the wide ranging discussion and debate and the demand for direct comparability that a conference setting might have allowed.

The primary units of analysis are also different. While Diamond and Fei take the natural village as the primary unit, Siu and Butler focus largely on the commune, with Butler tracing his study downward from the commune to its constituent brigades and teams and Siu tracing the administrative hierarchy upward, from the commune to the county. And the units chosen for analysis stand at substantially different levels of economic development. The village of Taitou analyzed by Diamond, for instance, has virtually no village level industries, while Huancheng commune described by Siu has industries so advanced that they are developing overseas markets.

What is therefore striking about these pieces is the extent to which they are comparable without any conscious attempt to make them so. And what this comparability suggests is that with more opportunities for interaction among field researchers, Chinese and Western alike, and more opportunities for field research, scholars would be in a much better position to describe and explain variability and similarity in Chinese society.

Differential Rate of Rural Development

At the heart of the four substantive pieces in this volume is a single underlying question: what explains the differential rate of development of Chinese villages? None of the authors deals explicitly with the apparently eternally vexing question of what, after all, constitutes development, but a range of implicit arguments are apparent. Fei Xiaotong, recalling his pre-Liberation studies, remembers that at that time he viewed the "hunger of the people" as the single greatest problem facing the Chinese countryside. Today, with the problem of hunger basically solved in Kaixiangong, and basic subsistence assured, the primary economic preoccupation of villagers is with improving their crowded housing. For Fei, development is directly tied to the material well being of the peasants, whose hierarchy of needs begins with food and proceeds to shelter.

Norma Diamond, implicitly at least, would agree with this hierarchy. While hunger per se is not a problem in Taitou village, the diversification of foodstuffs is, and Diamond posits a possible retrogression in this regard compared to the Taitou of pre-Liberation days described by Martin Yang. But Diamond notes the considerable improvement, and the consequent social implications, of the housing situation in Taitou, where the peasants today live in neat, new brick houses, comparable to the homes of middle-peasants of an earlier era, which in their design foster a living pattern of nuclear rather than extended families.

In Huancheng commune, where the problem of hunger is absent, Helen Siu focuses on commune level industries both as a measure of development and as an indicator of the successful implementation of the Chinese socialist ideal of overcoming urban-rural disparities. Fei and Diamond similarly point to the need for rural industries if rural development is to continue, and both tie that development directly to its potential for improving the peasant's standard of living. Steven Butler's approach to the problem of development here is more indirect, but he is no less interested than the other contributors in explaining why some villages develop more quickly than others. One of the questions he poses, impossible for Diamond and Fei whose unit of analysis is the village, is how or whether the commune has used its redistributive capacities to promote a measure of equality within and between villages. In a situation of scarcity, the question of equity becomes another measure of development.

The Local Impact of National Level Policy

Common to all the pieces included here is a recognition that national level policies as implemented in the rural areas have a major effect on the rate of rural development and on the quality of peasant life. While most of the authors view policy changes primarily in Chinese terms, as a progression from land reform, to mutual aid teams, to collectivization, to the formation of communes, Siu uses a cyclical model of policy change developed by G. William Skinner and Edwin Winckler,[23] positing regular and reasonably predictable alternating policy cycles within a longer term trend of secular development. Thus Siu, unlike the other authors, necessarily sees the current "liberal phase" as one that will give way to a more radical one.

That there is a relationship between national level policy and rural development is hardly a "discovery." Social scientists have been working with—and proving—that assumption for decades. What is most interesting about these pieces is their revelation that the same national level policy may have different developmental effects both on

---

23. See G. William Skinner and Edwin A. Winckler, "Compliance Succession in Rural Communist China: A Cyclical Theory," in Amitai Etzioni, editor, *A Sociological Reader on Complex Organizations* (New York: Holt, Rinehart and Winston, Inc., 1969) pp. 410-439.

Effect of policy

different villages and on different administrative and
economic units within the countryside. And under the same
policy, some indicators of development may rise while others
decline. Thus, whereas brigade level industries currently
being introduced in Kaixiangong under the new liberal
policies are having a remarkably salutory effect on peasant
income in the village, the same policies are having a
different effect on commune level industries in Huancheng
commune, compelling tighter administration by county-level
administrators with a subsequent loss of profit for the
commune and its constituent members. In Taitou village, while
the effects of the new liberal policies have been positive,
these policies have yet to be implemented with quite the
salutory effect as in Kaixiangong, leading Diamond to suggest
that constraints on economic development in Taitou emanate
not from the village itself but from policy decisions at the
higher, county level. Similarly, while Butler has yet to
analyze his data on the effect of current policies on income
disparities within and between teams and brigades, a likely
effect of current policies will be to increase those
disparities, with a consequent decline in equity.

What these preliminary findings suggest therefore is the
need for a more concerted focus both on the differential
effects of national level agricultural policy and on
differential levels of implementation. As commune industries
in Huancheng are losing profits to the county, are its
constituent brigades introducing brigade level industries,
the profits of which are then shared by the peasants? Are
the inequalities engendered by the new allocation of
responsiblities for agricultural production within production
teams and brigades outweighed by the increase in motivation
and subsequent overall increase in output? Can the different
effects of new agricultural policies on Kaixiangong and
Taitou villages be explained by different levels of support
at the county level for both the policies themselves and for
individual villages over which the counties exercise
jurisdiction? Are some villages better able to insulate
themselves from arbitrary commands from higher level
leadership than others? None of these questions are new, and
certainly they are difficult, but it is unlikely that they
can be answered without continued field research and a more
concerted effort at comparability.

The Rural-Urban Continuum

Another common theme of the pieces included here is the
importance to agricultural development of the rural unit's
position in the rural-urban continuum. Using the hierarchy

of regional systems developed by G. William Skinner,[24] Siu
identifies Huancheng as a periurban commune intimately tied
to the city and therefore very much affected not only by
shifts in policy towards agricultural areas but also by
shifts in policies directed toward urban centers.   In
contrast, Diamond describes the negative economic impact on
Taitou village of being artificially cut off from its natural
relationship to the urban center of Qingdao. Fei Xiaotong,
in future research on Kaixiangong, will also be examining the
relationship of the village to the city.

Rural Leadership

Finally, all the contributors to this volume mention the
problem of rural leadership, both within the units over which
leadership is exercised and in terms of relations between
lower and higher level leaders. Steven Butler was able to
interview officials at all levels of Dahe commune, and the
question of how that leadership adapts to a changing economic
and political environment is central to his study.   Norma
Diamond notes the relationship between the leaders of the
commune of which Taitou is a part and the leadership of
Huangdao district, suggesting that the excessive control
exercised by the district leadership over such questions as
land use, diversification of agricultural production, and
introduction of small scale industries has had a deleterious
effect on the potential development of Taitou. The "leftist"
error during the Cultural Revolution of arbitrary
bureaucratic command from the top by cadres unacquainted with
local conditions mentioned by Fei Xiaotong has taken longer
to correct in some places than in others. Helen Siu
similarly refers to the relations between commune and county
level leadership, suggesting that the pricing power of county
level officials (and their tendency to set prices low), as
well as the county's monopoly over marketing, cause
constraints at the commune level which lead in turn to
dissatisfaction and a loss of productive incentive. Fei,
too, mentions problems of leadership, focusing largely on
problems of education. Most village cadres have only a
primary school education and eschew further study because of
its perceived impracticality in terms of the daily production
and organizational demands of local leadership. Fei argues
that the task of China's educators is to insure that the
countryside receives modern, practical education with direct
applicability to the developmental tasks of the Chinese
village.

---

24. See G. William Skinner, editor, The City in Late
Imperial China (Stanford, California: Stanford University
Press, 1977).

The pieces included in this volume suggest the complexity of the many developmental problems facing the Chinese countryside. The editors of the volume hope that the reports included herein will also serve to demonstrate the potential value of continued field research both in identifying problems and in understanding the complex set of variables that determine whether, how, at what rate, and according to which indicators rural economic units will develop. Many of these questions simply cannot be investigated from the "outside," on the basis either of available documentary evidence or on the basis of reports from emigrees. Moreover, the determinants of development in a country as vast and differentiated as China can surely not be understood in all their complexity by generalizing from only a few cases. A sufficient number of case studies must first be amassed. Social science fieldwork is the epitome of what must be meant by the currently popular Chinese admonition to "seek truth from facts." Only further field research will reveal the full range of variables affecting Chinese agricultural development and how those variables interrelate.

Conclusion

In writing these concluding remarks, I am reminded of the hope expressed to me by one distinguished academic administrator at the Chinese Academy of Social Sciences, that the time has come for American and Chinese scholars to talk more about their similarities than their differences. The first sections of this introduction focused more on differences than similarities, not in order to broaden but to reduce the gap, to suggest the compromises, accommodations and adaptations the foreign field researcher may have to make in order to promote the success of his research. The second section, focusing on the substantive accounts contained herein, has focused more on the similarities than the differences. That the four scholars, one a Chinese, another a Hong Kong Chinese, the other two Americans, focus similarly on questions of the process of development in the Chinese countryside and identify remarkably similar variables in describing that process, is one indication that the barriers to scholarly communication may not be so great as is often assumed. Hopefully, these pieces will suggest the need for more, not less, interchange between Chinese and American social scientists and point to the fact that scholars from both countries have much to learn from each other.

That there are impediments both to increasing the level of field research in China and to further cooperation between Chinese and foreign field researchers cannot be ignored. These impediments have already been alluded to here.

In the final analysis, however, it is difficult for the Western scholar, even recognizing, understanding, and sympathizing with the ambivalence with which Chinese regard the question of field research by foreigners, to believe that more field research and greater interaction between Chinese and foreign field researchers could not but work to the long-term benefit of China's developmental goals. The differential effects of national level policy can only be understood "on the ground," through systematic field research in a well selected set of sites. Cooperation between Chinese and foreign scholars, including on-site training of Chinese field researchers by their foreign colleagues, offers a potential short-cut to the difficult process of rebuilding an indigenous Chinese social science. We hope that in the years ahead, both Chinese scholars and those officials ultimately responsible for questions of academic exchange, will come to agree.

2. Sociology and Anthropology in China: Revitalization and Its Constraints

In December-January 1979-1980, a delegation of China specialists, representing the Joint Committee on Contemporary China (of the American Council of Learned Societies and the Social Science Research Council) and the Committee on Studies of Chinese Civilization (of the American Council of Learned Societies), undertook a three week fact-finding mission to China. The task of the delegation was to assess the status of those humanistic and social science disciplines in which most American research on China takes place. I and my colleague, Martin Whyte, a sociologist at the University of Michigan whose evaluation of the importance of research in Hong Kong is included here, had the responsibility for reporting on the state of sociology and anthropology.[1]

Since that first fact-finding mission, I have also had the opportunity to spend six months in China conducting demographic research in a residential area of Tianjin city. My description of the current state of anthropology and sociology and my suggestions to potential future fieldworkers in China are based largely on my experiences during those two visits.

Chinese Sociology and Anthropology in Historical Perspective

Let me begin by placing the development of sociology and anthropology in China within an historical context. Sociology was introduced to China from the outside, largely from the West. Interest was initially spurred by the

1. For our report, see Martin K. Whyte and Burton Pasternak, "Sociology and Anthropology," in Anne F. Thurston and Jason H. Parker, editors, Humanistic and Social Science Research in China: Recent History and Future Prospects (New York: Social Science Research Council, 1980), pp. 148-163.

publication in Chinese of two translations. The first, in 1902, was Kishimoto Nomuda's Sociology, translated by Zhang Taiyan. The second, in the following year, was the translation of Spencer's The Principles of Sociology, by Yan Fu. Interest in sociology flourished thereafter, and by 1919 most Chinese universities had established sociology departments.

From the beginning, however, the Chinese notion of sociology was more eclectic than our own. It embraced parts of anthropology, demography, and even social work. One reason for this more comprehensive approach can be found in the sources of intellectual inputs into Chinese sociology. Both the Chicago school of American sociology and the British school of social anthropology affected the development of sociology in China. For this reason, the anthropological component of this hybrid Chinese discipline did not, with certain exceptions, include archaeology, linguistics, or physical anthropology—subjects which, in the United States, were then considered sub-fields of anthropology. The lines between sociology and anthropology were never very clearly drawn.

By the 1920's, the flow of sociological interest and debate had begun to follow a variety of new and exciting channels. While some scholars attempted to reinterpret Chinese society and history using analytic methods and principles derived from Marxism, others were inclined to use more traditional Western sociological perspectives and methods. Both approaches stimulated more general debate on the nature and destiny of Chinese society. Studies of the Chinese family, community, and society by both Chinese and foreign scholars proliferated, and these studies reflected both the vitality and diversity of the contending reformist and revolutionary schools of thought. Maurice Freedman has suggested that, by the beginning of the Second World War, "outside North America and Western Europe, China was the seat of the most flourishing sociology in the world, at least in respect of its intellectual quality."[2]

In 1949, however, the position of Chinese sociologists and anthropologists became a tenuous one. Their disciplines came to be regarded as unnecessary, and many scholars were suspected of having been corrupted by Western "bourgeois" thought and values. In 1952, with the national campaign to reorganize universities and colleges, the situation worsened dramatically. Sociology was officially declared a

2. Maurice Freedman, "Sociology in and of China," British Journal of Sociology, Volume 13, (1962), pp. 106-116.

"non-discipline," and departments of sociology were closed. For close to three decades, formal training in sociology and anthropology in China ceased. More than a generation of scholars and researchers were lost as a result.

Sociologists and anthropologists had no choice but to move into neighboring disciplines or to shift into entirely new lines of work. Quite a few found a niche for themselves in the Central Academy of National Minorities, established in Peking in 1951. But those who joined the National Minorities Academy also found it necessary to limit their interests and research to China's national minority populations, and to confine themselves to a type of research limited in its topics, technniques, and methods.

During the "hundred flowers" campaign of 1956-1957, some of China's leading social scientists proposed a revival of sociology, arguing that the discipline could be useful in finding solutions to important social problems.[3] The attempt at revitalization was soon frustrated. During the anti-rightist campaign of 1957, advocates of the re-introduction of sociology were branded as "rightists," and many of them dropped into immediate and lengthy obscurity.

Following the death of Mao Zedong and the fall of the "gang of four" in 1976, China's political leaders adopted a different position. They began to suggest that social science knowledge might in fact serve important practical purposes, that such knowledge might provide information useful to China as the country began its climb out of the rubble and chaos engendered by the "ten year catastrophe" of the Great Proletarian Cultural Revolution (1966-1976). With official blessing, sociology began a modest, cautious recovery.

Ironically, some of the people now giving breath to the spark and feeding this small fire are the same scholars who had been branded as rightists in 1957. The task they have taken upon themselves after nearly three decades of "darkness" is a formidable one indeed. Resources necessary for disciplinary growth and development are less adequate now than in the 1920's, and the constraints on development are tighter. On the other hand, the intellectuals who are guiding this venture are a lot wiser now than they were then.

---

3. See, for instance, Fei Hsiao-t'ung, "A Few Words on Sociology," Wen-hui Bao (Shanghai), February 20, 1957, translated in James P. McGough, editor, Fei Hsiao-t'ung: The Dilemma of a Chinese Intellectual (New York: M.E. Sharpe, Inc., 1979), pp. 32-39.

Chinese social scientists today find themselves in an unusual position. Policy makers are listening to them to a degree unparalleled at any other time since the establishment of the People's Republic. Social scientists, for the moment, are in a position to have at least an indirect influence on policy. But the political basis underlying the revival of sociology has implications for the way the discipline is likely to develop. Chinese officialdom now stresses that truth should be derived from facts rather than from political dogma, and the new sociology-anthropology is expected to be principally policy-oriented, focused on providing results of practical relevance to the "four modernizations."[4] Chinese authorities now openly admit a number of domestic problems, problems that in their view are residues of the Cultural Revolution — growing signs of excessive self-indulgence among the young, rising rates of juvenile delinquency, higher levels of unemployment, serious housing deficiencies, instabilities arising from changing intrafamilial relationships, problems of management and incentives, and the perennial problem of overpopulation, for example. Chinese authorities and scholars devoted to the revival of sociology hope that the discipline will be able to inform policies designed to deal with these problems. In this sense alone, there is a political channelling of purpose behind the development of the discipline.

The development of sociology is politically constrained in another way as well. While scholars are encouraged to borrow widely—from the United States, Japan, Eastern Europe, and even from the Soviet Union—they are also being urged to develop an unambiguously indigenous version of their discipline — to import methods and techniques without either becoming dependent on foreigners or contaminated by their "bourgeois" ideologies and values. To the extent that students are presented with foreign methods and ideologies, such ideas must also be presented in such a way as to avoid political and ideological contamination.

Given both the scarcity of trained researchers and teachers and the limited resources available for training and development, Chinese colleagues will find it difficult to fulfill the pragmatic mandate set for them. That mandate would be difficult to meet even if China did have a pool of trained personnel and abundant resources. Isolating foreign methods and concepts from their ideological contexts will also prove difficult, although in a practical sense it may be sufficient if new techniques and methods simply appear to be

---

4. The "four modernizations" are of industry, agriculture, science and technology, and the military.

Chinese. And if research turns out to be ineffective, or if research conclusions challenge official commitments and assumptions, critics may once again come to question both the usefulness of such research and training and the political motivations of those involved.

Problems also arise from within the scholarly community itself, where longstanding and deep-rooted intellectual, pragmatic, personal, and political differences sometimes generate considerable tension. Deep-rooted differences within the Chinese intellectual community can serve to frustrate, divert, or possibly even to halt disciplinary development. While such tensions are certainly not unique to China, they are particularly acute there. Chinese scholars have become adept at functioning in a milieu fraught with both subtle and not-so-subtle antagonisms, but having to function in that milieu is akin to swimming upriver burdened with stones. Foreign colleagues dealing with Chinese counterparts must remain ever sensitive to the fact that the difficulties faced by their Chinese colleagues are not merely practical but personal and political as well.

The Revitalization of Sociology and Anthropology

China's new sociological life was inconspicuously sparked in 1978, when Hu Qiaomu, then president of the newly established Chinese Academy of Social Sciences (CASS), called a meeting of scholars previously associated with anthropology and sociology to discuss the question of "rehabilitating" the discipline. Of the senior scholars invited to attend the meeting, some understandably greeted the idea of revitalization with no great enthusiam. A few actually stayed away from the meeting, and others remained frankly skeptical about whether the time was yet right to begin planning the reintroduction of sociology.

In 1979, Hu Qiaomu asked the noted social anthropologist, Fei Xiaotong, to call a second meeting. It was only at this time that most of the participants agreed that some modest, tentative efforts should begin. A major outgrowth of this meeting was the establishment, in March 1979, of the Chinese Sociological Research Association, which took as its task efforts to stimulate field development. Since that time, the national level Sociological Research Association in Peking has been actively pressing for the creation of academic departments within the Chinese university system, research institutes within local academies of social science, journals, and the like. Sociological Research Associations (or Sociological Associations, as they

are sometimes called) have now been established at the
municipal level in Peking, Shanghai, and Tianjin
municipalities and on the provincial level in Hubei,
Heilungjiang, and Jilin provinces.

Another important outgrowth of the 1979 meeting was the
creation, in 1980, of a separate Institute of Sociology
within the Chinese Academy of Social Sciences—in addition to
the older Institute of Nationalities, which continues to
exist. Because the new Institute of Sociology still operates
with meager resources in terms of personnel, funds, and
space, its activities are largely confined to field
development and to building an institutional infrastructure
for field development. Active research has only recently
begun.

The institutional framework begun in Peking has now
expanded substantially. Today, every province and
municipality in China has a social science academy of its
own, and within a few of these academies, sociology
"institutes" or less formal sociology "groups," preparatory
to the establishment of institutes, have already begun
functioning. The Shanghai Academy of Social Sciences has
such an institute, for example, although it is technically
termed "provisional" pending formal municipal approval. But
this provisional institute already employs some 30 people,
and is divided into six "research groups," in sociological
theory, middle and old age, childhood and adolescence,
marriage and the family, labor, and a data-documents group.
The research group on marriage and the family is conducting a
major study of divorce in Shanghai.

The Institute of Social Sciences in Heilungjiang also
has a functioning sociology group, and the Jiangsu Academy of
Social Sciences has recently decided to establish a
full-fledged sociology institute. Preparations for it are
already underway, pending formal provincial approval. Within
still other provincial and municipal social science
academies, people have clearly expressed an interest in
establishing sociology institutes or groups. But all these
structures are still in an incipient phase of development,
with activities and research still in the planning or
exploratory stage.

While field development is considered the most urgent
task at the moment, neither the national level Chinese
Sociological Association nor the Institute of Sociology at
the national level Chinese Academy of Social Sciences are in
a position to direct that development, either in the
provinces or in China's universities. Provincial and

municipal level social science academies are controlled by provincial or municipal level authorities, while the' universities fall under the jurisdiction of the Ministry of Education. These are distinct hierarchies—different administrative grooves—which, in China, are very difficult to bridge. As a result, the influence of the national level Sociological Association and the Institute of Sociology is largely informal and fraternal—a product of support from the national level political leadership on the one hand and the persistence and development of personal relationships with colleagues in the provinces on the other. The importance of this administrative limitation should not be underestimated. As will be seen shortly, in the discussion of recent attempts to separate anthropology from sociology, scholars in the provinces do not always heed the advice of their colleagues at the national level.

Practical Constraints

The proliferation and development of sociological institutes and associations is severely limited by serious deficiencies of formally trained personnel, funds, and space, as well as by the virtual absence everywhere of basic library resources. It is also limited by a lack of the kind of foreign language proficiency that would make it possible for Chinese scholars to use foreign reading materials, even were such materials widely available.

While shortages of research materials and inadequate foreign language preparation continue to pose major obstacles to the development of sociology and anthropology in China, the most serious problem is undoubtedly the shortage of trained teachers and researchers. How can universities and research institutes staff a discipline where there has been no formal academic training for nearly thirty years?

The Chinese are using imaginative means to deal with this problem. One of the major tasks of the sociological research associations has been locating older people formally trained in sociology and anthropology before 1952 and encouraging those still capable of teaching and research to return to active service. The talents of people whose work during the past few decades has provided them with related practical experience are also being tapped. And several crash training courses have already been conducted, as much to stimulate interest and support for continued development as to provide training. These courses were designed to bring the older generation of scholars a bit more up-to-date as well as to recruit and expose younger scholars to new possibilities.

Training Workshops

These training efforts began very modestly. In 1979, during his visit to the United States as part of the first delegation of Chinese social scientists and humanists to visit since before Liberation, Fei Xiaotong invited several foreign scholars to lecture in Peking. During the summer of the following year, a formal, two-month training program in sociology was provided in Peking by scholars from the University of Pittsburgh and from the Chinese University of Hong Kong. Focusing on basic sociological concepts, social statistics, and the sociology of modernization, the course was attended by about forty people (not including many auditors) from all over China--social scientists, researchers, university professors, applied social workers, and a few journalists. Because reaction to this first formal program was so positive, a more ambitious one was offered during the summer of 1981. Drawing again upon scholars from the University of Pittsburgh and the Chinese University, as well as from Boston University, this course focused on short introductions to a greater variety of topics: community analysis, social psychology, social research methodology, sampling and analysis, demographic statistics, cultural anthroplogy, and the sociology of knowledge. In addition, Chinese scholars lectured on such topics as scientific socialism and historical materialism. The students, around fifty in all, were similar in composition to those who had attended the first workshop.

These training workshops were intended to serve several purposes. Apart from basic training, its organizers hoped to stimulate a nation-wide interest in sociology and closely related disciplines. With students drawn from all over China, it was hoped that the seeds of interest planted in Peking would be carried back to grow in provincial soils throughout the country. The organizers also hoped to adapt the lectures presented during the training course to new, indigenous textbooks, suitable for use in China's academic environment. Finally, organizers hoped that successful completion of these first ventures would generate conditions suitable for further disciplinary development. The programs were painstakingly designed with the realities of the Chinese situation in mind and, for that reason, these training courses were largely successful in fulfilling their stated purposes.

Formal Academic Training

In addition to these short training programs, and apart from the proliferation of associations, institutes, and work groups, there has been another important institutional development -- the re-emergence of formal academic training. In 1979, a group of scholars originally associated with the Department of Politics at Fudan University's Branch Campus in Shanghai set up China's first new sociology department. The new department began with 28 undergraduate students from the former Department of Politics. Three more classes were subsequently added by national examination (in 1979, 1980 and 1981), and there are now 134 students in the Fudan program.

In February 1981, China's second academic program in sociology was begun at Nankai University in Tianjin city within the Department of Philosophy. About 43 applicants from universities throughout China were selected to take part on a formal basis—to complete their senior year studying sociology. In addition to Nankai faculty and Chinese scholars from elsewhere, a number of foreign lecturers have periodically contributed to this endeavor. Ten or so students from the program have been selected to continue for an additional two or three years of graduate work in sociology at Nankai. The others will be assigned jobs where they will be able to make use of their new interests.

In February 1982, the Department of International Politics at Beijing University also established a program in sociology.[5] Six students selected by national examination have begun graduate work in this program; another six will go to a similar one expected to be in place soon at Zhongshan University in Canton.

In a major departure from the tendency in the north to focus on the re-establishment of sociology, a separate department of anthropology has already been established at Zhongshan University. Departing substantially from the British model, the Zhongshan anthropology department aims at integrating cultural anthropology, archaeology, linguistics, and physical anthropology in the American fashion. It already provides undergraduate training in the first two of these sub-fields. Linguistics and physical anthropology will be added in 1983. For reasons to be outlined shortly, this effort could have far reaching significance.

Plans to establish still more academic programs and courses in sociology and anthropology are also under way. Colleagues in Peking note that by 1982, some 60 or so young

5. Judging from recent reports, the sociology courses offered at Peking University are extremely popular, one of them having more than 500 students. See "Higher Education," Beijing Review, Volume 26, No. 4 (January 24, 1983), p. 30.

people received some formal training at Nankai and Beijing Universities alone.   It may soon be possible to send some of these people abroad for further training. By 1984, a core of fully trained teachers of sociology-anthropology should be back in China.

The development of academic courses and programs will involve herculean efforts for some time to come.   The problems are many. Administratively, for example, it is no simple matter to shift faculty from one university (or even from one department) to another.   Universities and their constituent departments, like government agencies, are very resistant to the transfer of quality personnel, and no one can be transferred without the permission and cooperation of the unit in which he already works. Some of those whom universities and research institutes would like to tap have long held jobs outside an academic setting, and securing their release can involve lengthy and sometimes unsuccessful negotiations. Where programs emerge from within existing departments, struggles over resources and assignments are to be expected. An even greater problem is that many of the people designated and willing to teach have relevant experience but little or no formal academic training in sociology or anthropology, and few have had systematic research experience. These people are being asked bravely to hold the line—to serve as bridges until a new generation of people can be formally and systematically prepared to replace them. And they must do this job without adequate library resources, classroom texts, or the kind of foreign language training that would enable them to draw upon the work of foreign scholars (and thus to avoid the temptation to reinvent the wheel). At the same time, they have been sensitized to the risks of over dependence on foreign scholars.

Source Materials

Many libraries were destroyed or dismantled during the Cultural Revolution, and Western textbooks and monographs remain in very short supply. Such textbooks and monographs that are available are often outdated. In the acquisition of books and other reading materials, the social sciences generally have lower priority than the natural sciences.

Moreover, preparing suitable readings for students poses a particularly thorny problem. The difficulty is not simply one of unstocked libraries and inadequate language preparation, although these deficiencies are certainly part of the problem. Obtaining permission to publish in the present Chinese context involves a time-consuming, difficult procedure in the course of which many different editorial judgments are made, often by people whose interests and expertise lie elsewhere. As a result, publication is not only slow, but uncertain. During the review process, so many diverse revisions may be required that the version finally published may have a thrust quite different from that originally intended. Many manuscripts never get that far.

Despite the difficulties and pitfalls of the Chinese publication process, Chinese sociological texts are being prepared. Ten teachers drawn from among participants in the 1980 summer training program are writing a basic sociology text, drawing together materials from the workshop, earlier Chinese articles, and selected translations. This volume is expected to be approved for classroom use by 1983. Additional texts, covering some of the topics included in the second summer training program, are also under preparation. During my recent research stay in China (1981-1982), I came across a number of other sociological materials in Chinese -- a text on social statistics based on a course offered by a foreign scholar at Nankai University, an introduction to sociology written by a scholar on Taiwan, and a dictionary of sociological terms published in Hong Kong, for example. But these materials are not yet considered appropriate for general circulation or for classroom use.

The problem of deciding what should and should not be translated for general classroom use is also a vexing one. This question is as much political as it is economic and academic. Given the present fragility of sociology-anthropology in China, and given continuing tensions both within the academic community and between the academic community and the state, the preparation of classroom materials must be approached with considerable caution. At this stage, painful compromises may be necessary simply to ensure continued disciplinary growth and development.

Training Abroad

In addition to the various training efforts being carried out in China, a few people have also been sent abroad. Our Chinese colleagues are currently more interested in training than in degrees, and have therefore been willing to send a few middle-aged scholars overseas for a year or two, in addition to sending younger ones for longer periods. The older people will return sooner and are expected to have sufficient background to enable them to protect, cultivate, and prepare younger scholars to spend longer, more formal periods of training abroad. Since there is no middle generation of scholars senior or influential enough to protect and direct the growth of this fragile flower, these brave people will have to serve as best they can as a temporary bridge between generations.

But in the short term, there are limits to what the Chinese can hope to accomplish through formal, foreign training of scholars. Overseas training, even for those in a non-degree status, takes time. More importantly, Chinese priorities preclude anything but the most modest investment in overseas training for anthropologists and sociologists. Anything beyond the most limited opportunities for such study will, to a large extent, depend on the willingness of foreign institutions to make fellowships and scholarships available to Chinese students, some of whom will have less than optimal preparation.

Research Efforts

While training a new generation of scholars continues to have top priority in China, modest research efforts are nonetheless already underway.

That branch of anthropology known in China as "national minorities studies" is carried out primarily in a number of specialized academies and research institutes located throughout those parts of China with substantial minority populations. Because China's minority populations are often located in peripheral and strategically sensitive areas closed to foreigners, and because published research from these areas is difficult to obtain, foreign scholars have limited knowledge of research efforts in national minorities studies. Some scholars who have spent many years in national minorities areas are now returning to urban centers, and a few have even been sent abroad for further study and research. It is my suspicion, however, that most people doing research in this area will, for some time to come, continue to concentrate on editing and publishing materials acquired during the massive field investigations conducted from 1956 to 1963.

Apart from these continuing activites, though, there are other research efforts of a new and different sort. An attempt to develop a variety of permanent "research stations"—in rural communes, urban neighborhoods, factories, and in other settings throughout China—has already begun. Workers at these stations will receive training as they gather basic descriptive data on the one hand and conduct more analytic studies on the other. Their work will focus primarily on pressing social problems. Several stations are already in place and others will be soon. Peking has an urban station with four researchers, and the Department of Sociology at Fudan University is operating another in Shanghai. The Institute of Sociology of the Shanghai Academy of Social Sciences is preparing to open a second urban station in that city. The urban research I conducted in collaboration with Chinese colleagues in Tianjin city will also be continued under the auspices of a new research station there, as a project of the Tianjin Academy of Social Sciences. And, as Fei Xiaotong notes in his piece in this volume, the village of Kaixiangong will house a permanent rural research station.

There are signs that colleagues in Peking are beginning to think now about consolidating and integrating the work of these separate research projects. There is talk of better, more limited, and more relevant problem definition and about encouraging a degree of compatibility between stations in terms of problems researched and methods used. A nationwide meeting of the Chinese Sociological Research Association was held in April 1983 to begin planning coordinated research efforts and to develop priorities for research in the coming five years.

The Boundaries between Sociology and Anthropology

One aspect of the re-emergence of sociology and anthropology in China may well cause confusion and misunderstanding in the West. The problem arises from the way the Chinese define the boundaries of sociology. In China, these boundaries have important implications both organizationally and in terms of access to resources. Chinese social anthropologists are no longer wedded to the structural-functional tradition that once characterized British social anthropology, but neither have most of them shown an interest in moving toward the kind of American anthropology that integrates cultural anthropology, linguistics, archaeology, and physical anthropology. One possibility is that the thin line between sociology and social anthropology that formerly characterized the field in China will become thinner still. But some recent developments suggest a move in a different direction--toward more diversified development.

Since 1979, when the field of sociology began to find new life, a number of key people once identified with national minorities studies have shifted back into sociology. During our discussions in China in 1979-1980, Whyte and I detected a certain rivalry between the people remaining in national minorities studies and those shifting into sociology--a competition in some instances exacerbated by past personal and political differences. Some Chinese anthropologists may choose to identify with the new sociology and to draw a sharper line between themselves and those who continue to study China's national minorities—or rather the history of China's national minorities, since these people seem reluctant to deal with contemporary populations. If this continues, anthropology as a discipline could become more fragmented than before in China.

On the other hand, there are people who clearly would like to see a less restricted form of anthropology emerge as a separate discipline in China. A report in <u>Minzu Yanjiu</u> (<u>Nationalities Research</u>) in May 1981 notes that 91 "professors and anthropological workers" from 18 provinces in China met recently at Xiamen University in Fujian and spent six days listening to papers and discussing the status of anthropology. Also discussed were the differences and natural affinities between cultural anthropology (<u>wenhua renlei xue</u>) and ethnology (<u>minzu xue</u>). Developments such as this, plus the establishment of a new department of anthropology at Zhongshan University, suggest an active movement toward separate disciplinary identity for anthropology. Given the location of both developments, the energy driving this movement may be concentrated in China's southeastern provinces. I have yet to detect signs of support or encouragement for this thrust in the north. In short, the relationship between sociology, cultural anthropology, ethnology, national minorities studies, physical anthropology, linguistics, and archaeology seems even less clear now than when I visited China in 1979. I would therefore be less confident than I was then in predicting that China is on the road to a truly integrated sociology-anthropology. The small sound that signalled new sociological life earlier now resonates on many frequencies, but that fact alone might well be the best indication of growing confidence, vitality, and viability.

Foreign Fieldworkers and Their Constraints

It was within the context of developments just described that limited opportunities for fieldwork in China by foreigners began to open up. While many sociologists and anthropologists had made short visits to China after 1972, usually riding piggyback on delegations sent for other purposes, there had been few opportunities to remain in China long enough to conduct formal, longer term fieldwork. Since the normalization of relations with the People's Republic of China in January 1979, several foreign scholars have been able to undertake long-term fieldwork—the first such ventures in about thirty years. Scholars began to go for substantial periods of time and, initially, were permitted to remain in specific locations long enough to conduct systematic research. A few were even permitted to conduct reasonably long-term fieldwork in several sites in sequence. This was no small accomplishment, given the history of Chinese-American relations and the atmosphere within which Chinese sponsoring agencies must function. For a while, it seemed as though serious, systematic fieldwork by foreigners would finally be possible and that the possibilities might gradually expand with a deepening of the new scholarly exchange relationship.

But from the beginning, the Chinese have shown considerable reluctance to accommodate foreign scholars. While constraints on what researchers could do and on where they could conduct fieldwork were loosened considerably following normalization, fieldwork by foreigners remained a delicate, sensitive matter—one that required patience and flexibility on both sides.

The initial phase of optimism changed suddenly in January 1981, when Chinese officials began to announce, to every visiting delegation that would listen, that for a "short period of time," during which China readjusted to the legacy of chaos left over from the Cultural Revolution, fieldwork by foreigners could no longer be accommodated. Given the massive economic and social rearrangements then being implemented, the Chinese argued, the diversion of attention, personnel, and resources to accommodate foreign researchers would be "inconvenient." Some suggested that with the changes being introduced in China, a certain measure of disorder was likely, thereby rendering it difficult to guarantee the safety of foreign fieldworkers. Nonetheless, the Chinese coupled the assertion of inconvenience with assurances that the suspension ought not to be seen as a step backward, or a closure, but merely as a temporary measure, to remain in effect for a couple years. Moreover it would still be possible, in the interim, for some researchers to come to conduct fieldwork for shorter periods of time -- two to three weeks.

Two additional reasons must be mentioned for the suspension of fieldwork. First, because of its sensitivity, fieldwork remains more ⸲vulnerable to political shifts in Sino-American relations. Thus, during the delicate period of discussions and negotiations over possible sales of sophisticated weaponry to Taiwan, the termination of fieldwork was sometimes tied by Chinese to the political difficulties engendered by possible American arms sales and to longer-term issues of the whole "Taiwan question." In

addition, the publicity in the American press given to al-
leged excesses by one former American fieldworker in China[6]
— described by Anne Thurston in the introduction to this
volume — lent credence to those in China who were arguing
that the foreign presence in China was already excessive.
The fact that fieldworkers necessarily "delve deeply" into
Chinese society renders fieldwork particularly vulnerable to
political shifts and to concerns about the dangers of foreign
presence.

As of this writing, the prospects for future fieldwork
in China remain uncertain. The Chinese, as noted in the
introduction, are still reviewing a set of guidelines
governing such fieldwork, guidelines that must be approved by
national and local level government and Party organizations
before the current suspension is rescinded and foreigners are
once again permitted to carry out fieldwork. The content of
those guidelines and what effect they will have is still
unknown. One the one hand, it is possible that high level
approval for fieldwork by foreigners will ease the tension
that local levels must inevitably feel in hosting foreign
researchers. A more likely possibility is that the
guidelines will be so constraining as to preclude many types
of field research, and that Hong Kong and Taiwan will remain
essential, important research sites for many years to come.
For this reason, the inclusion in this volume of Martin
Whyte's assessment of research at China's gate, in Hong Kong,
is especially useful.

From August 1981 to February 1982, after the suspension
of fieldwork by foreigners in China came into effect and
after the other foreign researchers who have contributed to
this volume had completed their research, I was permitted to
conduct research in Tianjin city as part of an agreement
worked out with the Institute of Sociology at CASS prior to
the moratorium. And several other foreign scholars also seem
to have been able to conduct fieldwork after the imposition
of the moratorium. But whatever the content of the new
guidelines currently under discussion in China, it is
doubtful that the constraints under which I worked will be
eased. Although my own research—a social demographic study
of an urban neighborhood—could be adapted to those
constraints, the constraints were such as to preclude
certain other types of fieldwork. I could live with the
restrictions imposed on my research because my project did
not require continuous, unimpeded contact. An anthropologist
with more traditional ethnographic goals would undoubtedly

---

6. See "Trouble for a China Hand," *Newsweek*, November 2,
1981, p. 113.

have found such restrictions on access more incapacitating. For the present, as Norma Diamond also observes, projects involving "participant observation" are likely to be most difficult for the Chinese to accommodate, and the researcher should be prepared to make painful compromises.

In anticipation that some forms of fieldwork will still be possible if the new guidelines are promulgated, and recognizing that there are as yet no real "models" to be emulated, let me nonetheless venture some very concrete suggestions to future fieldworkers who may be contemplating a plunge into Chinese waters. By outlining the process whereby fieldworkers are placed in China and the constraints under which they work, other potential fieldworkers should be better able to understand the limitations of fieldwork in China and to decide for themselves whether those limitations are worth the effort.

Affiliation and Placement

The people who report here on their field research in China used different modes of entry. Butler's research was sponsored by the Committee on Scholarly Communication with the People's Republic of China, and the Chinese Academy of Social Sciences provided him affiliation and arranged his research. Diamond carried out research during breaks from teaching at Shandong University, and the arrangements for that research were made by provincial level foreign affairs authorities with cooperation from university officials. Siu negotiatied access privately, but again with the permission and cooperation of provincial level authorities in Guangdong. Negotiating permission to carry out research will remain the most difficult stumbling block for some time to come, and for potential researchers without particular institutional or personal ties in China, the most probable route of access will remain the Committee on Scholarly Communication with the People's Republic of China (CSCPRC). The CSCPRC serves as both funding and negotiating agency, and its extensive ties with academic institutions within China allow it to pursue a variety of potential access routes on behalf of people it sponsors. With one route blocked, the Committee can still pursue others.

On the other hand, with increasing personal and inter-university ties between China and the United States, the possibilities for individuals to negotiate access privately are also expanding. Since routes of access are so particularistic, let us assume that the drama of placement has been played out and that you managed to receive your visa in time to make your scheduled flight to China. You have passed the most important hurdle, but the hurdles that will ultimately determine the success or failure of your research have yet to be passed.

Shortly (often <u>very</u> shortly) after your arrival, your hosts will meet with you to discuss your "requirements," to review your research design. While you may have arrived with the impression that your requirements had already been negotiated and re-negotiated in painstaking detail, you will return at this point to "square one" to negotiate your proposal again. These negotiations are more than mere formality. In my judgment, they begin the most critical phase of your fieldwork.

Your hosts are likely to begin these discussions by outlining their constraints and problems in such discouraging detail that you may be tempted to conclude that you made a mistake in coming at this inconvenient and difficult time. Avoid the temptation to make reservations for the next flight out. If you begin with some understanding of their concerns and limitations, your hosts will in all probability be more sympathetic to yours. A dialogue will follow during which you can work out a way to carry out your research responsibly but realistically--in terms of the constraints within which the Chinese must operate.

It is important to understand why arranging fieldwork projects is such a complicated and time-consuming procedure. Your official hosts in China, whether the Chinese Academy of Social Sciences or a university, cannot require a locality to receive you. Placement can be accomplished only after considerable legwork and persuasion involving a host of people and several levels of the bureaucracy, from the municipality down to the residents' committee or the province down to the commune. Before permission to receive you is granted, your hosting agency will not only have made numerous phone calls but will have sent a representative to the locality to argue on behalf of you and your project. If your project is flexible enough to be carried out in a variety of locations, placement will be easier. In my own case, for instance, a number of localities rejected my project before the Tianjin municipal authorities, the Tianjin Academy of Social Sciences, and Nankai University agreed to receive me.

In this regard, let me observe that the most unkind thing your hosts could possibly do would be to point you toward a locality, hand you a travel permit, ticket, and letter of introduction, and send you on your way. Such a procedure could not possibly work to your advantage. It is essential that you leave the details of placement to your hosts. Moreover, you should be prepared to allow a month or slightly longer for the completion of the placement process. A placement made too hurriedly will almost certainly be less effective than one made carefully and completely at the start.

Many provinces have indicated that for the present, they will not receive any (or any more) foreign fieldworkers. One reason for this is simply that local officials have more important things to do—more pressing undertakings and more directly rewarding ways to use their resources. Chinese frequently refer to the present period as one of "readjustment." In fact, however, the term is euphemistic. One does not need to live long in China to sense the profound effect of the Cultural Revolution on the social fabric. The policies currently being implemented in China represent a major break with the past, and the host of administrative problems involved suggests that the last thing most local administrators need right now is a "foreign guest."

Compounding these administrative concerns is the pervasive Chinese preoccupation with national security, and the possible implications of a foreign presence for that. There is a general suspicion of foreigners in China, one that has deep historical roots, but one that has been particularly nurtured in recent years. Accommodating a foreign fieldworker runs counter to the norms with which Chinese administrators work.

There are two important implications for project planning in the difficulties of placing researchers in the field. First, if you have designed a project that can be successfully carried out in a variety of different locations, you will give your hosts greater leeway as they work on behalf of your placement. Once they understand the type of unit in which you would like to work, they will begin to contact possible local sponsors — agencies where they have friends, or students, or former colleagues.

Secondly, given the machinery and the times, choosing a research project that focuses on one site rather than on several is likely to be better received, better set up and arranged, and more effectively implemented. Making complicated arrangements in one place is certainly less of a burden than having to make them in several places, and remaining in one place will allow you time to develop the kind of rapport that will engender cooperation. It is better, for the present, to pick a problem and project that is not so complicated to arrange that it will frighten off potential local sponsors.

In addition to remaining flexible with respect to research site, it is also important to arrive in China with a research design that is as flexible as possible -- one that can be readily adjusted to current possiblities and limitations. It would be a mistake to arrive with a plan so burdened with detail as to be impossibly constraining. If the nature of your project is too constraining, you will exceed the capacities of the Chinese to accommodate you, and it might be more prudent to wait for better times.

Research Design and Specifications

On the other hand, once you have understood, through your discussions with your hosts, what their limitations are, it is important that the research specifications you present to them be as specific and straightforward as possible. During the course of your negotiations, you will be asked to draw up, within one or two days, your list of research specifications. This document should not cover the background or theoretical implications of your research but should go directly to the heart of the project. You should state, in a few pages, what you want to do, what specific data you will require, and, if applicable, the specific questions and topics to be discussed with respondents.

There are two reasons for being as specific and straightforward as possible. First, your sponsors will use this document in negotiating your placement with local authorities. It is important that they understand the basic purpose of your research very clearly so they are able to present your case convincingly to these officials.

Second, this document will become a *tigang*, a formal outline, which, as Butler points out, will take on the function of a contract once your research has actually begun. Once your *tigang* has been accepted by local hosting authorities, your flexibility will decrease dramatically. Any subsequent modifications or deviations from the formal outline will probably require a new series of negotiations. You will have to send a letter to your sponsoring agency explaining what you want to do, why, and the relationship of this request to the basic project goals as outlined in the *tigang*. Your sponsoring agency must then approve those changes, which can take time. If the sponsoring agency does approve, it will then send down a *pishi*, a formal request, to the local authorities encouraging them to accommodate this new specification. There is no guarantee that the local authorities will agree to this change, but without formal approval, local approval is highly unlikely. Moreover, because it is so difficult to move from one administrative groove to another in China, requests for data controlled by agencies outside the ones with which you are working are especially difficult to negotiate. While in Tianjin, for instance, I thought it would be useful to have data on height and weight measurements from a local elementary school just across the street from my office. But the school was run by the Ministry of Education, and I was working with the municipal and street governments under sponsorship from the Chinese Academy of Social Sciences. Such a request would have had to go up to the Chinese Academy of Social Sciences in Peking, over to the Ministry of Education in Peking, and down to the local school in Tianjin. I decided against making the request.

The difficulties involved in modifying the tigang do not mean that modifications are impossible. Both Butler and I were able to make some modifications during the course of our work. If one avoids burdening one's sponsor with too many requests and if it is clear that the request is reasonable and within the bounds of the original specifications, the request is likely to be honored. But such changes do take time and add to the administrative burdens of one's hosts.

On-Site Constraints

Several of the contributors to this volume note the constraints under which they worked in the field. Norma Diamond was not permitted to live in the village, for instance, and both the necessity of "commuting" and discouragement from local officials prevented her from engaging in the casual interchange upon which anthropologists thrive. Butler notes that initially he was not allowed to jog alone in the morning, that someone was always sent to accompany him in case something "went wrong." Both point to the lack of privacy during their interviews and to the problems that situation posed. Such constraints are likely to persist.

Chinese notions of hospitality, and their concern for the personal comfort and security of their guests (as well as for their own comfort and security during your residence) can be excessive. But it is unlikely that any foreigner will be able to persuade his hosts to modify these attitudes substantially. Here is one of many junctures at which our trains often pass each other in the night. Your hosts will feel as strongly about finding you suitable housing, food, and climate as you may feel about not being pampered, isolated, or needlessly constrained. There is a temptation to overreact and thereby to run the risk of allowing the good will that has been built up to vaporize in an instant. If one goes to China expecting to find intrigue, isolation, surveillance, and constraint, one will surely find them. The question is whether we allow such expectations to divert us from the research goals and interests that drew us to China in the first place.

The municipal authorities in Tianjin agreed to permit my research only after I had agreed to constraints similar to those described by some other contributors to this volume -- if I would agree to live in a hotel rather than in the residential area in which I would be working; if I would agree not to ride my bicycle through the city to work each day; and if I would agree to conduct my interviews (with older women) in an office provided by the street government rather than in the homes of my respondents.

There was an instinctive temptation to balk at these stipulations. Had I done so, however, I might have jeopardized the entire research project. I therefore quashed my instincts and agreed to all three stipulations. Then we agreed on a compromise. Realizing the financial burden living in a hotel and riding a cab to work and back each day would impose, my hosts found much less expensive housing for me on the campus of Tianjin Universtiy. They worked out a way for me to have lunch at my office so I would not have to go home "to rest" each afternoon. Finally, they negotiated a special fare for regular car service morning and night.

The stipulation that I could not conduct interviews in homes did not change, however, although I did periodically visit and interview people in their homes at their request. Given the nature of the demographic data required for my project, the research itself was not hampered by this stipulation. In fact, because the street committee was responsible for setting up my interviews and keeping a steady flow of respondents coming to my office, my work proceeded more quickly and smoothly this way. But the argument that interviews in homes would impose upon informants the additional burden of having to clean house in anticipation of my visit is not entirely persuasive. Others considering fieldwork in China should be aware that this constraint is not likely to change and projects where participant observation is vital are not likely to be met with favor.

There is another unpleasantness that deserves mention, one that sometimes goes away if one is around long enough. Both Diamond and Butler describe the difficulties of conducting interviews in the presence of numerous observers -- cadres sent from one's sponsoring agencies and various levels of local government. The explanation usually given is, that these people represent responsible agencies and are there "as a matter of courtesy as well as of interest." This kind of courtesy and interest can be ruinous to a good interview. The experience of some has been that these visitors eventually tire of it all and stop coming—and clearly that is more likely if one is around for a while. While Chinese academic authorities are becoming convinced that this attention is counterproductive and, therefore, not appreciated, solving the problem is not easy. Academic sponsors simply have no power to insist that other responsible agencies refrain from sending people to interviews. Requests to that effect can be made, but it is not certain they will be honored in each instance.

The fieldworker should anticipate a variety of other seemingly pointless restrictions. On occasion for instance, I was discouraged from taking certain photographs because they might "create a bad impression." I was also told I could not take my original, working questionnaires out of China but that I could take my final forms, which contained precisely the same information. Foreign fieldworkers should be forewarned that data collected collaboratively may be used by the Chinese in their own research and the fact that such data was gathered collaboratively may not necessarily be noted in Chinese publications.

Finally, there is the matter of privacy, of which there is precious little in China. There is usually no way to seal oneself off and no way simply to melt into the population. For the foreign fieldworker accustomed to privacy, this fishbowl existence is potentially the most difficult constraint he will face. Over time, the lack of privacy can become exhausting and debilitating, and in this frame of mind, reactions to trivial frustrations can be exaggerated. It is a problem with which all foreign researchers will have to cope.

Assistants and Colleagues

Of crucial importance to your project will be the kind of person assigned to work with you. This person will remain with you throughout your field research to facilitate your work in the field. The job calls for someone with intelligence, political sophistication, determination, and coolness. He or she must clearly understand and be interested in what you are doing, and the foreign researcher should take pains—considerable pains—to inspire such interest. Finding such people is difficult. Where institutes or universities have them, they are often reluctant to divert them from important business to our needs, especially if our research goals seem irrelevant to those of our sponsors. But without a competent assistant, the foreign researcher faces a difficult situation. The Chinese would like to be able to use our visits as an opportunity to train their people, but they are often unable, at present, to spare precisely the people who would be most likely to benefit from such training and cooperation.

Some of us have openly wondered why, with China's unemployment problem, foreign fieldworkers are not allowed simply to hire whomever they choose. My own experience has convinced me that, were we allowed to do so, the result would probably be very disappointing. The success of my research was vitally dependent upon the assistance and cooperation of people at three levels: the colleague assigned to work with me by the Chinese Academy of Social Sciences, the colleague assigned by the Tianjin Academy of Social Sciences, and the representatives of local residents' committees. Even my very able colleagues from CASS and the Tianjin Academy had their hands full negotiating their way into the local scene. The academic credentials of my colleagues from Peking and Tianjin could not have compelled the local cooperation necessary to conduct my interviews. Representatives of the residents' committees had to prepare the way.

Let me illustrate the problem very concretely. Once the Tianjin municipal government had agreed to host my project, the municipal authorities then had to spend time finding and persuading a street government to receive me. The street cadres then had to prepare the people through whom they work to help me. They had to explain why I was coming, what I wanted to do, and why it was important that they spend time and go out of their way on my behalf. That meant meetings with the elected representatives of the two residents' committees (each representing about 500 households) in which I would be working. These representatives in turn convened meetings of their "small group" leaders, and so it went right down to the door of each potential informant. Each new request I made meant a new set of meetings. Arranging for questionnaires to be distributed and collected, arranging revisits to correct them, and arranging for people to be where they were supposed to be at the right time similarly took endless legwork and time. To have hired someone without official affiliations and well established contacts would have assured that the research got nowhere.

When some of the work we were doing became overwhelming, I thought of hiring some unemployed local people to help us on a temporary basis. Street cadres and my own colleagues talked me out of the idea. It was impractical on several grounds. If I started directly compensating people for extra help, where would it end? What about the residents' committee representatives and the small group leaders, and the people from the Tianjin Academy of Social Sciences who regularly helped us in innumerable ways? It would open a pandora's box. More important, these hired people would be outside the street and residents' committee structure and, for that reason, would likely be refused cooperation. I worked in Tianjin long enough to know that this advice was sound, and Butler's description of being assigned an assistant from the commune in which he worked suggests that a similar situation prevails in the countryside. It may be inefficient in terms of research needs, but it is a given of the Chinese system that no foreign researcher can change.

The Fieldworkers' Responsibilities in China

While in the field, the foreign fieldworker may be visited from time-to-time by Chinese scholars passing through or by people from one's sponsoring agency who drop in to see how things are going. These are occasions to build important bridges, and such visits should not be considered intrusive, even if they are sometimes inconvenient. Steven Butler describes such a visit by a representative from CASS, during which Butler was both able to assure the CASS representative that his project was going smoothly and publicly to thank the local officials responsible for the project's success.

You will likely be asked to lecture several times during your stay in China. So long as these requests do not get out of hand, this is one way we can be responsive to Chinese needs and, at the same time, reduce apprehensions about the presence of foreign researchers on Chinese soil. Foreign fieldworkers should come to China prepared to lecture on the general state and nature of their discipline and speciality.

The foreign field researcher is almost invariably asked to present a final lecture just before leaving, and should be prepared to present a preliminary report on his findings in the field at that time. The last obligation should be taken very seriously. It deserves considerable preparation and attention. How one's research findings are presented will affect whether the Chinese judge the project a success which, in turn, is likely to have a bearing on the reception of those who will follow.

There is a final point to be made—about the foreign field researcher's responsibilities to others who may wish to follow him or her to the field. However much we may wish to

be treated solely as individual researchers, we are
nonetheless viewed as representatives of our disciplines and
of all—or most—potential fieldworkers. The Chinese know,
or are learning, that we all have different personalities and
different styles of operating in the field. For that very
reason they can be expected to remain wary of granting access
to individuals whom they have not yet come to know and trust.
But any field researcher in China also stands as a
representative of those to follow. The cooperation and
success of today's fieldworkers can render the path of those
who may come later just a little bit smoother. If, over the
years, we can develop a history of projects that both sides
mutually judge successful, then the inevitable failures will
seem less jarring, and both sides will be able to build on a
firmer research base and with a measure of confidence more
complete than currently exists.

3. On Studying China at a Distance

During the years when it was not possible to carry out sociological research within China, and while sociology was a proscribed discipline in that country, a great deal of research was carried on from the outside, "at a distance." Fairly involved methodologies have been developed to cope with the problems of this type of research. Now, sociology is being revived in China, and a small number of Western researchers, including several contributors to this volume, have been able to conduct field studies within China. The time seems ripe for a preliminary assessment of the art of studying China at a distance. Are the approaches and methods used in this kind of research ones that can and should be abandoned now that possibilities for conducting field research in China are increasing? Or are there valid reasons for continuing this type of research as a complement to research within China? I will try to answer these questions here. My assessments must of necessity be preliminary. The "honeymoon period" of academic exchanges with China, at least with respect to field research, is over, and it is unclear once the current "moratorium" on field research is lifted either what kinds of research will be feasible within China or what sorts of constraints may be imposed on researchers.

The first step in such an assessment is to describe the major modes that have been used in studying China at a distance. Systematic sociological research on Chinese society has generally used one of four types of data, singly or in combination: refugee interviews, newspaper accounts, literary texts, and reports of visitors to China.[1] Which type of approach a researcher uses depends upon his topic and resources, and some topics are more readily studied using one

---

1. See Michel Oksenberg, "Sources and Methodological Problems in the Study of Contemporary China," in A. Doak Barnett, editor, Chinese Communist Politics in Action (Seattle:

kind of data than another. For example, for analyzing elite attitudes, newspaper or literary sources are quite useful, while refugee interviews are of little value. For analysis of the internal dynamics of grass roots social units, refugee interviews are far superior to the other modes. Since refugee interviewing is the mode that can be most clearly seen as a substitute for field research within China, and since it is the mode with which I am most familiar, the remainder of this paper will focus on the advantages and disadvantages of this type of research at a distance, concluding with a tentative balance sheet of the value of refugee interviews versus the value of field research within China.

Hong Kong Interviewing

A few words must be said about the general procedures employed in refugee interviewing. Virtually all such research has been conducted in Hong Kong, and most of the scholarly interviewing in Hong Kong has been carried out through the Universities Service Centre, an institution funded by American foundations which provides scholars from many parts of the world with office space, excellent library facilities, and a base from which to make the contacts that interviewing entails. The procedures for conducting refugee interviewing are fairly simple to specify. The researcher arrives with a topic to study and devises an outline of questions or topics to discuss with a sample of refugees. The usual pattern is to have intensive, semi-structured interviews based upon a standard outline, rather than to use a questionnaire. And the refugees serve not as respondents in an attitudinal survey, but as informants about the social units in which they lived and worked within China. Often the researcher hires Chinese research assistants to help locate refugees and sometimes to conduct interviews or to serve as an interpreter in the interviews. No method has been devised to select a systematic sample of the refugees arriving in Hong Kong, and of course the refugees themselves are not representative of the population still living in China. Researchers can assure themselves of some variety in the people they interview, however, by placing a suitable newspaper ad or instructing research assistants to screen potential informants according to various background characteristics: age, sex, regional origin, occupation, and

University of Washington Press, 1969); and Martin King Whyte, "The Study of Mainland China: Sociological Research and the Minimal Data Problem," in Contemporary China (March 1977), pp. 1-12.

so forth. Researchers have varied in their approach to numbers. Some have looked for one or a few especially well-informed people and have then interviewed them at great length to construct case[2] studies of particular organizations or social realms in China. Others have interviewed dozens of people, each for more modest amounts of time (say, 10-15 hours, rather than hundreds of hours) and have then presented composite pictures of[3] social organization or comparisons of different social units.

Interviews typically require several sessions, often of about three hours each. A variety of procedures are followed to try to get full and accurate information from informants: assurances of privacy and anonymity, description of research purposes, questions designed not to be leading or threatening, a focus on concrete personal experiences and observations, and steering clear of directly inquiring about political attitudes or conveying one's own attitudes. The general practice has been to pay informants for their time and trouble (for a number of years the "going rate" was HK$15 per hour or approximately $2.50 U.S. per hour), although if one interviews fewer informants for longer periods of time it may be possible to establish a more personal relationship and not use the potentially embarrassing hourly payments. Some researchers tape record their interviews and then have them translated and transcribed later, while others simply take very detailed notes and type up an interview report from these soon afterward. The tradeoff seems to be whether the researcher feels the extra detail from the tapes is worth the extra time and expense involved in transcribing everything and the danger of extra anxiety that some informants feel when speaking with a tape recorder going.

---

2. For example, A. Doak Barnett, Cadres, Bureaucracy and Political Power in Communist China (New York: Columbia university Press, 1967); Gordon A. Bennett and Ronald N. Montaperto, Red Guard (Garden City, New York: Doubleday, 1971); and Marc J. Blecher and Gordon White, Micropolitics in Contemporary China (White Plains, New York: M.E. Sharpe, 1979).

3. For example, Victor C. Falkenheim, "Political Participation in China," in Problems of Communism (May-June 1978), pp. 18-32; B. Michael Frolic, Mao's People (Cambridge, Massachusetts: Harvard University Press, 1980); William L. Parish and Martin King Whyte, Village and Family in Contemporary China (Chicago: The University of Chicago Press, 1978); and Martin King Whyte, Small Groups and Political Rituals in China (Berkeley: University of California Press, 1974).

Since in a typical interview session various topics in the outline are covered in only a rough sequence, with new lines of inquiry pursued as they arise, the time between such sessions gives the researcher time to go over the transcript and check for topics on the outline that have not yet been covered fully, as well as to check for areas of vagueness and inconsistency that should be probed in the next interview. If an informant should turn out to be unsatisfactory for one reason or another—for example, if he or she does not match the desired background characteristics, is uncooperative, inaccurate, or simply vague—then the researcher can simply decide not to invite that informant back for subsequent interviews and can disregard the information provided.

There are a number of procedures for at least partially checking the accuracy of refugee accounts. Some information can be checked against stories in the Chinese press, and some against the accounts of other informants. Informants can also be asked probing questions in follow-up sessions to see whether their stories remain consistent and clear. In some cases, other people who know or have interviewed the informant can be asked for judgments of his or her credibility. Still, many details from an interview represent personal experiences that are difficult to verify from other sources, and for this reason relying too heavily on any one informant can be a risky procedure.

Researchers then make use of their interviews in their scholarship in a variety of ways. Some use the interview material as their primary data and subject it to detailed analysis, as in the studies cited earlier. Others use interviews as supplementary information, designed to throw added light on the documentary or other data which serve as the primary source of information.[4]

Problems in Hong Kong Interviewing

There are a number of basic problems in refugee interviewing that make it less than ideal as a research

---

4. Richard Baum, Prelude to Revolution: Mao, the Party, and the Peasant Question, 1962–1966 (New York: Columbia University Press, 1975); Thomas Bernstein, Up to the Mountains and Down to the Villages: The Transfer of Youth from Urban to Rural China (New Haven: Yale University Press, 1977); Charles P. Cell, Revolution at Work (New York: Academic Press, 1977); Ezra F. Vogel, Canton under Communism (Cambridge, Massachusetts: Harvard University Press, 1969); and Lynn T. White, Careers in Shanghai (Berkeley: University of California Press, 1978).

method. Some of these can be compensated for and corrected, while others must simply be accepted as given. Here I will describe what some of the most important problems are, and how they are generally handled.

The problem most frequently raised is the issue of bias. The common statement is "if these people decided to leave China, surely they must have an anti-communist bias and will give a distorted view of Chinese society." This is a less severe problem than is often assumed. First, most refugees are not committed anti-communists. They come to Hong Kong for a variety of reasons, most often having to do with their search for greater personal opportunities, and many retain strong patriotic sentiments toward China and admire many aspects of the society they have left. For instance, in comparing the quality of interpersonal relationships in China and in Hong Kong, informants my colleague William Parish and I have interviewed almost universally see China as far superior.[5] Second, by avoiding sensitive issues and questions of political attitudes, and by focusing on organizational specifics and personal experiences, the interviewer can confine the interviews to areas where personal biases are less likely to have much influence. Third, there is substantial variety in the backgrounds and orientations of refugees, and if a sufficient number of diverse people are interviewed, the researcher can qualitatively or even statistically check whether those expected to be more anti-communist yield different accounts, and correct for this factor.[6] Finally, as mentioned earlier, there are ways to check the accuracy of at least parts of the information supplied in an interview, and these can be used to screen out seriously biased informants.

A related concern is over the question of "professional informants." This is expressed in phrases such as, "aren't you likely to get people who make a career out of being interviewed by researchers, people who become adept at telling foreigners what they want to hear, rather than what

5. See also, Perry Link, "Refugees in Hong Kong," Harvard University Papers on China (December 1969), pp. 1-19.
6. The statistical procedures are described in the methodological appendix in Parish and Whyte, Village and Family, op. cit., and carried out throughout that volume. These procedures derive from the "quality control" procedures used in cross-cultural research within anthropology, and they involve examining data and relationships constructed from the interviews and then partialling out various background characteristics of the informants one at a time to see whether the results are affected.

China is really like?" Again we have not found this to be a
real problem. In recent years there have been a large number
of refugees flooding into Hong Kong, while there are only a
few researchers doing scholarly interviewing at any one time.
These researchers may be looking for quite different kinds of
informants and want to interview them for only a limited
number of hours. So being interviewed is not something out
of which a person can make a career, although of course it
may provide desirable extra income when one is getting
settled or between jobs. By proper checking on the
background and integrity of informants and by proper
reassurances of the limited nature of the interviews, we have
found it possible to avoid concern over the so-called
professional informant.

In many ways, a more serious problem than bias is the
issue of selectivity. As noted earlier, no way has been
devised to sample all refugees in Hong Kong systematically,
and refugees themselves are not in any sense representative
of the population left in China. In recent years, there have
been two rather distinct groups of refugees arriving in Hong
Kong, each with its own skewed characteristics. The illegal
refugees are the type that has long been the staple of Hong
Kong interviewing--people who escaped from China, most often
by swimming or in boats. A disproportionate share of these
illegal refugees come from Guangdong Province, adjacent to
Hong Kong, and they tend to be younger, better educated, more
often male, and of class backgrounds less likely to stand
them in political favor than the general population in that
province. In recent years, many of the illegal refugees have
been urban youths who had been "sent down" to the countryside
in the late 1960's and 1970's, although urban workers,
peasants, and other groups are also represented.[7] The
legal refugees are people given exit visas by the Chinese
authorities. They are almost all people who had returned to
China from abroad and then decided to leave again, or people
born in China who had overseas relatives. Unlike the illegal
refugees, they come from all over China, but they also tend
to be relatively well-educated and predominantly urban, and
their overseas connections generally give them higher incomes
and a separate status from the rest of the population within
China.

The selective nature of the refugees available presents
a number of problems for researchers, as Helen Siu also notes
in her article in this volume. First, the availability of
different types of people is contingent upon policies
followed by both the Chinese and the British authorities.

---

7. See Bernstein, Up to the Mountains, op. cit.

Until about 1972, legal refugees came into Hong Kong in only a trickle, so that interviewing projects had to rely primarily on illegal emigrants. Since that time, legal emigration has mushroomed, with about 150 arriving per day in 1980. British policies have fluctuated between virtually no effort to control the flow of illegal refugees (in 1962 and again in 1973-74) and a "touch base" policy, which means that refugees will be sent back to China if they are caught en route. If they can reach Hong Kong and find a haven among kin or friends, however, they can stay. But faced with an estimated 150,000 illegal refugees arriving a year in 1979-80, a new stricter policy was announced in October 1980 under which any illegal refugee detected[8] anywhere in the colony would be sent back to China. There have also been efforts by colonial authorities to get the Chinese to cut the flow of legal refugees to fifty a day or fewer. Obviously, the more restrictive the policies of the authorities toward emigration, the more difficult it is for researchers to locate and interview refugees.

The skewed nature of the refugees available at any point in time means that researchers have to adapt their topics and questions to the kind of people likely to be available. Generally speaking, it is easiest to interview about common areas of social life about which many people are likely to have knowledge--schooling, neighborhood organization, village life, and so forth. It is obviously not very feasible to use such interviews to research topics such as elite politics and factionalism at the national or provincial level. Even research on some local aspects of Chinese society can be quite difficult; for example, dealing with local military or Party organization, or with life in minority areas. Still, the very large number of legal and illegal refugees coming into Hong Kong in recent years has allowed researchers to be selective in picking people to interview, and to find people from a fairly broad spectrum of geographical and social backgrounds. In particular, the legal refugees include enough doctors, accountants, engineers, and other professionals to research topics that would have been difficult[9] in the earlier days of interviewing those who had escaped.

But one still has to be careful to take into account the influence that the skewed nature of the refugee sample may

8. Details provided by John Dolfin, Director of the Universities Service Centre, Hong Kong.
9. Jerome A. Cohen, "Interviewing Chinese Refugees: Indispensable Aid to Legal Research on China," Journal of Legal Education (October 1967), pp. 33-35.

have on the picture one gets of Chinese social organization. Several approaches are commonly used to deal with this problem. One is to ask informants to supply information not so much about themselves and their families, but about close neighbors and co-workers, people still in China, who are not likely to be as atypical as the informants themselves. Again it is generally advisable to interview a fair number of people from different backgrounds. By so doing, one can hopefully screen out or compensate for the selective views provided by any one particular type of informant. Still, refugee interviewing can only provide information about areas of life with which the people available for interviews have personal experience, so the coverage of various areas of Chinese social life will remain spotty, and a number of kinds of research remain difficult or impossible. For instance, one cannot readily decide to research a particularly interesting work unit or village about which one has read in the press. Nor could one do the types of village studies described in this volume. But one can study villages, factories, or hospitals in general.

Another set of difficulties concerns problems of memory, although this problem to some extent is common to most research based on interviewing. Since informants are being asked to report "at a distance" by recalling earlier experiences, it is easiest to find relatively "fresh" (i.e. newly arrived) refugees and interview them about current or recent matters. On the other hand, it is more difficult, although not impossible, to use informants as sources of information about events and experiences back in the 1950s. Younger informants will not have had such experiences, and older informants may have only vague recollections. Even about relatively recent events informants may have problems recalling such things as specific policies and practices and time sequences. For this reason, it is again desirable not to rely too heavily on one informant, and to compare other interviews and press accounts and even to use these to jog the memories of informants.

A related problem involves the limitations of informant accounts. Respondents will in the course of an interview volunteer many unexpected bits of information, but successful interviewing still depends upon substantial advance preparation and knowledge on the part of the researcher in order to ask the right questions. If one doesn't know enough to inquire about a certain matter it may not be volunteered, and by not being on the spot in China and able to view the scene, many interesting lines of inquiry may be omitted. For example, in research with William Parish on patterns of rural change we were initially unaware of the traditional existence of "youth houses" in many Guangdong villages.[10] Perhaps two-thirds of the way through our project, mention of them was made, and in later interviews we inquired about them and found they were still fairly widespread, but by then it was too late to go back and check with our earlier informants on whether they still existed in their villages as well. As a result, we missed a chance to collect systematic data on regional variation in the persistence of this interesting institution. If we had done our homework more thoroughly, or if we had been able to live in a village with "youth houses" for any length of time, we would not have missed this topic.

Another set of problems stems from the limitations of verbal reports as a source of information about human behavior. There are a number of important aspects of social life that are quite complex and subtle, and therefore hard to get a clear picture of through interviewing. We have found, for instance, that it is quite difficult to interview people about methods of childrearing, husband-wife relationships, and similar topics, without ending up with very hazy and not very enlightening answers. These are difficult areas to study through direct observation also, to be sure, but the Hong Kong interviewer continually finds it frustrating not to be able to view the scenes being described to him.

Social life consists not only of organization, customs, and behavior, but also of components such as attitudes, values, and emotions. However, it is very difficult to get a rounded picture of matters such as these in Hong Kong interviews. In fact, the quest for objectivity requires the interviewer to steer away from inquiring about attitudes and emotions directly, in order to minimize the influence of any informant biases. To draw any conclusions about popular motivations and values, one is forced then to infer such things from the evidence provided of people's behavior, and to make use of whatever spontaneous clues are volunteered in the interview. But interviews are a much better source of data on how things work and how people behave than on how people feel about life.

A final shortcoming of Hong Kong interviewing is of quite a different type. This type of research is obviously conducted according to the researcher's own goals and priorities and does not form part of a research effort involving communication and collaboration with Chinese social scientists, and thus it does not provide an opportunity for

---

10. See Parish and Whyte, <u>Village and Family</u>, <u>op. cit.</u>, pp. 231-232.

the researcher to enter into a dialogue designed to lead to greater understanding about that society. In the past, with sociology banned within China, one could console oneself with the thought that such collaboration was impossible in any case. Now that sociology is being revived within China, the fact of working in isolation in Hong Kong rather than as part of a collaborative research effort within China is obviously unsatisfying in many respects.[11]

Advantages of Hong Kong Interviewing

Arrayed against these problems in refugee interviewing in Hong Kong are a number of advantages that also should be taken into account. I discuss these in relation to the available alternatives, particularly field research within China and the analysis of Chinese press accounts.

The first point to be made about Hong Kong interviewing is simply that it is a flexible technique that allows one to learn much more about the actual patterns of social life than any of the other methods that have been used to study China "at a distance." Chinese press accounts tend to be filled with exhortations and model examples, telling us more about how things are supposed to work than about how they actually do work. Even when problems are described, they tend to be only selected problems that the leadership wants units to confront and handle in specified ways. And many aspects of social life are never described in any detail in the mass media at all. If one relies on this source, then, one gets a one- or two-dimensional picture of Chinese society, one in which most of life revolves around whether people are complying with policy A or directive X or not. Much the same can be said of the kind of picture one gets from briefings on trips to China.

Through Hong Kong interviewing, whole new worlds of Chinese social life open up to us. We can learn rich details about daily life experiences and inquire about areas rarely discussed in the press. How does rationing work? What determines which middle school urban children attend? How do people now celebrate traditional festivals? Who gets the bonuses and pay raises in a unit and why? How is the garbage collected? From the sublime to the ridiculous, we can roam around in the recollections of our informants and eventually

---

11. Some other problems related to research in Hong Kong are not discussed here. The major one is simply the cost. Rents in Hong Kong, in particular, have risen so high that it is becoming very difficult to stay there for any length of time.

arrive at a fuller, three-dimensional picture of the patterns of Chinese social life. We can learn how certain policies were actually carried out in various settings, as opposed to the way they were supposed to be carried out. We can discover the many other features of social life that influence people's lives in addition to current government policies. We can hear details of popular satisfaction and fulfillment and of frustration and anguish. We will find the rich descriptive details in our interview transcripts laden with colorful anecdotes, wry observations, and dramatic personal experiences. Once researchers have become "hooked" by engaging in Hong Kong interviewing, they find it very hard to go back to studying China by reading between the lines in People's Daily, even in its modestly enlivened current form.

   With a bit of extra effort and ingenuity, Hong Kong interviews can provide more than simply rich, ethnographic-type information about Chinese social life. It is possible to use interview information to construct a variety of kinds of samples that can then be used to carry out the kinds of systematic comparisons that are the main tool of sociological analysis in other societies.[12] This must be done with caution, of course, for one has to take into account the selective nature of the group of informants one interviews. But it is possible to use interviews to construct a crude sample of villages, work units, schools, or urban neighborhoods to compare. And one can elicit information from informants about neighboring households, local cadres, weddings attended, divorce cases, local crimes, and other matters, and use these to construct additional samples for comparative analysis. Using such methods, it is possible to examine issues such as variations in leadership backgrounds, change in marriage behavior over time, the correlates of mobility opportunities, the sources of differences between male and female wages, and many other important matters. Using these kinds of internally constructed samples, a wide range of questions that never seemed tractable by any method "at a distance" can be addressed.[13]

---

12. See the discussion in Whyte, "The Study of Mainland China." op. cit.
13. For details and examples, see Parish and Whyte, Village and Family op. cit.; and Martin King Whyte and William L. Parish, Urban Life in Contemporary China (Chicago: University of Chicago Press, forthcoming).

Interviewing in China

But what about the comparison between Hong Kong interviewing and fieldwork and interviews within China? Doesn't the opportunity for fieldwork present many of the same advantages just discussed without many of the problems and headaches of work in Hong Kong? The contributors to this volume who have already conducted field research describe the variety of their research experiences in some detail. From my perspective, there seem to be a number of problems that make research in China also far from an ideal situation. Perhaps the circumstances will change for the better, but there appear to be aspects of the China research setting that count in favor of Hong Kong interviewing, at least for some topics.

First, as Steven Butler describes in some detail, the researcher must have a project and research method that can run the gauntlet of Chinese sensitivities and bureaucratic approval procedures. Some topics that are quite mundane may nonetheless be seen as threatening by Chinese authorities --perhaps folk religion or ethnic conflict, for example. In other topic areas, there may be no suitable research institute or other institutional sponsor with which to affiliate. Access to many field sites seems to require long and difficult negotiations. And there is often still a preference to locate foreigners in "model" sites, although the contributors to this volume seem to have been able to overcome that problem. The sort of research sociologists often find most advantageous, involving real research stays (rather than short visits) in several different locales or organizations, chosen according to the researcher's own criteria, seems extremely difficult to arrange. All of these considerations mean that sociologists and others wishing to pursue research in China presently must be prepared to adjust their topic and approach to fit within a variety of constraints. Of course, there are understandable reasons why foreign researchers should not be able to go wherever they please in China and study whatever they wish. And there are good arguments to be made in favor of trying to aim for collaborative research possibilities with Chinese social scientists, rather than demanding one's own way and going it alone. However, American researchers tend to be independent-minded and individualistic, and many will find that for certain topics, the less constrained research environment in Hong Kong is still preferable to a stay within China. Approval for research in Hong kong is easily obtained (visas are sponsored by the Universities Service Centre) and does not require complex, bureaucratic screening.

Part of the comparison involves the simple issue of

uncertainty. At this stage the range of research possibilities within China is not entirely clear and may improve. However, there is still a certain "gamble" involved in setting off to do research in China. Experiences to date seem to vary widely in how productive they were, and scholars continue to fear that, even if their project is approved, they may turn up in China and find their efforts continuously frustrated by bureaucratic and other obstacles. And of course the entire research exchange process remains to a considerable extent "hostage" to domestic politics within China and the state of Sino-American relations. Research access in some cases has apparently been granted reluctantly only after the application of pressure from higher levels, in order to serve current normalization goals. The danger remains that such access could be quickly cut off, or drastically reduced, if these larger political factors change. For Western social scientists with only a limited amount of leave time from teaching, and with pressures to continue to generate research and publications, the uncertainties involved in China research at the present still involve some risk, at least in many topic areas. In contrast, the research situation in Hong Kong is more stable, and one can have a clear idea in advance of what one can and cannot do there. So in the near future, at least, this is a factor likely to count in favor of Hong Kong interviewing.

Another difficulty concerns the interviewing situation within China. Thus far, as Norma Diamond and the introduction note, it is very difficult to arrange the kind of confidential interview setting that is essential to research and which can be obtained in Hong Kong. I gather that the Chinese often prefer to bring designated people to the researcher to be interviewed or to have guides or others accompanying the researcher when he sets out to conduct interviews, the latter situation being described in Steven Butler's article here. Even if one could arrange for interviews directly and carry them out privately, however, in such a tightly controlled society as China, those interviewed would not be able to melt back into the social landscape anonymously as they can in Hong Kong. The possibility of an informant being questioned later about what was asked, and the replies given, clearly makes the China interviewing situation more constrained than in Hong Kong. People are speaking more freely in China these days, even to foreigners, but it still seems unlikely that ideal interviewing conditions are attainable. Chinese who might take the initiative to seek a foreigner out and volunteer information are likely to be more atypical than the sort of people one can find to interview in the crown colony. Given these limitations on interviewing within China, at least one

foreign researcher who was living in China for an extended
period of time found it desirable to have interviews
conducted for him in Hong Kong at the same time.[14] For
some topics, of course, lack of confidentiality in the
interviews in China would not be a major problem, but the
idea of people tailoring their research and questions to fit
within Chinese constraints does not seem entirely healthy.

There are potential advantages to interviews in China in
terms of being able to do things that sociologists elsewhere
take for granted, things that are not possible in Hong Kong
conditions. This concerns in particular being able to draw
systematic samples, as Burton Pasternak was able to do in
Tianjin, and to collect survey-type data on popular
attitudes. Same public opinion polls have begun to appear in
China, conducted by the Communist Youth League and other
agencies, but Chinese social scientists are just beginning to
acquire and utilize the required research techniques. For
the time being it seems doubtful that many Western
researchers will be able to carry out or even participate in
survey research within China, and of course the same sorts of
problems about confidentiality and interview bias affect this
sort of research as well.

One additional consideration in favor of Hong Kong
interviewing should be mentioned. Over the years a
considerable research apparatus and multiple channels of
information about Chinese society have been built up in Hong
Kong. Without this infrastructure Hong Kong interviewing
would not be half as fruitful as it is. In Hong Kong the
researcher has access to excellent library facilites of the
Universities Service Centre, the press clippings files of the
Union Research Institute, the Western and Chinese library and
periodical collections at Hong Kong University and the
Chinese University of Hong Kong, and also potential contacts
with other researchers, businessmen, diplomats, journalists,
and other interested parties, as well as access to the
Western press. Impressions gained in interviews and by
reading the press can be set in a context gained from all of
these other sources. No such comparable set of research
facilities and information sources exists within China.
Therefore, depending upon where the researcher is located, he
or she will be cut off from some of the most useful
information and sources. Of course there are compensating
sources of information within China, as well as the ability
to check impressions by personal observation, but, depending
upon the topic, these may not fully compensate for what is
lost.

---

14. See Frolic, Mao's People, op. cit.

One of the potential advantages of research within China is professional collaboration. Although many western research projects to date have been individual projects, an increasing number of them have begun to involve at least limited collaboration with Chinese social scientists, and hopefully fuller collaboration will develop in the future. The prospect of being able to discuss research problems with Chinese colleagues is attractive indeed, as is the idea of playing a role in the interchange of ideas and research techniques between Chinese and Western social science. The chance to play some role in the development of Chinese social science fits well into the "missionary impulse" that inevitably seems to form part of American culture, even if this impulse sits less well with Chinese host institutions and colleagues.

However, it is well to recognize that there are potential dangers here as well. Does one have to "pull one's punches" in what one writes in order to protect collaborators within China and for fear of creating problems for later researchers? If the political winds change again in China, are the Chinese researchers who worked with you likely to suffer political problems? Little as yet has been published as a result of the research exchange, but questions such as these are a source of concern for many. Clearly, if it turns out that one can do productive research within China but then cannot freely and fully report the results then the value of China research in relation to Hong Kong interviewing will come under question. Perhaps it is not a fair precedent to cite, but one of the few really collaborative projects carried out in scholarly exchanges with the Soviet Union resulted in the American researcher feeling he had to submit his manuscript for very detailed criticism and editing by the authorities in the Soviet institution with which he had collaborated, in order to protect his colleagues there.[15] Clearly this represents undesirable constraints on the Western researcher. The mood in China at present is more objective and self-critical than in the past, and if this spirit continues to develop and stabilize, and if a sufficient appreciation of the aims and orientations of Western researchers develops to smoothe over Chinese sensitivities, then perhaps these worries will be unfounded. Until the water is tested, though, the isolation and lack of collaboration in Hong Kong may be seen as advantages, for if there is no cooperation involved, then there are no agreements and persons who might be jeopardized.

---

15. Urie Bronfenbrenner, Two Worlds of Childhood: U.S. and U.S.S.R. (New York: Pocket Books, 1968).

In general, then, if one looks at Hong Kong interviewing in comparison with the potential problems and constraints of fieldwork within China, several things count in favor of sustained work in Hong Kong. One is less constrained there by Chinese bureaucratic obstacles and political sensitivities, both in what one studies and in what one writes, although there are other kinds of constraints in Hong Kong which were discussed in the first part of this paper. One can locate in Hong Kong a range of people from different regions and walks of life to get a broader view of social reality than can be generally arranged within China, although one cannot study particular organizations and sites at will. One can conduct interviews in a much more confidential and unrestrained manner, and as a consequence the frankness and fullness of the information supplied are likely to be superior. One can also utilize the considerable research apparatus and multiple channels of information that have been built up in Hong Kong. One can determine fairly precisely what kinds of research one will be able to do, and one does not have to worry that what one writes will cause problems for organizations and individuals within China. For some topics none of these considerations will loom important, while other factors may make Hong Kong unsuitable as a research site. But in at least some areas, Hong Kong interviewing continues to have advantages that more than compensate for the short-comings of this method that I discussed earlier.

Conclusions

Drawing up a balance sheet at the end of this exercise is not an easy matter. It clearly makes no sense to say that research in Hong Kong is preferable across the board, nor for that matter is research within China. Two conclusions do suggest themselves. One I have already alluded to: whether one chooses to go to Hong Kong or to China for research depends a great deal on the nature of your topic and the methods you propose to use to research it. If the project concerns areas of social life that are likely to be part of the experience of a fair number of Hong Kong refugees, but entail sensitivities or a research design that would be hard to arrange, then Hong Kong will be preferable. On the other hand, some kinds of projects--research on a particular factory or village, for example--generally cannot be done from Hong Kong, and when personal observation of subtle relationships and visual details is important, then obviously a China research stay is preferable.

The second conclusion is that these two approaches should not be seen strictly as alternatives, for they can complement each other. If the researcher has time and resources, in many cases the best approach may be to combine both, optimally by a stint of Hong Kong interviewing before going to conduct research in China. Steven Butler indicates in his article here that his research in China benefitted from prior research in Hong Kong, and Helen Siu argues the virtues of using Hong Kong as a research base. One of the potential problems of research in China is that a great deal of preparation and background knowledge are necessary in order to make the best use of one's stay there. Often useful information will not be volunteered, but will only be supplied if the researcher inquires and knows what to probe for. General reading about China and following the Chinese press may not provide the kind of detailed background desirable. A previous stint of interviewing in Hong Kong can be used to advantage in a number of ways. Through interviews one can begin to penetrate below official slogans to learn how things actually operate. This knowledge can be used to design a research strategy and focus areas of inquiry so that less time in China has to be spent familiarizing oneself with the basic features of local social organizations. By interviews with a varied Hong Kong sample, one will acquire the perspective to be able to judge how typical or unusual a particular work organization, village or other site within China really is. This sort of detailed knowledge and awareness will generally make it easier to get down to brass tacks with collaborators and informants within China, and to get more detailed and forthright responses to questions. At the same time the greater appreciation of the texture of Chinese social life one can gain from Hong Kong interviews should enable one to live in China with less "culture shock" than would otherwise be the case. A number of scholars have already been following the approach of combining Hong Kong interviewing with fieldwork within China (e.g. Deborah Davis-Friedmann, Steven Butler, Victor Nee, Helen Siu, Ezra Vogel), and those with whom I have spoken feel that without this prior preparation their work in China would have been much less productive.[16]

In the future it seems clear that research on China "at a distance," and Hong Kong interviewing in particular, will not occupy as central a place as in the past. However, this type of research has by no means become outmoded or

---

16. The idea of putting in a stint of interviewing in Hong Kong _after_ a research stay in China is not considered here, and seems less useful. One could still use Hong Kong interviews to gain a clearer sense of whether the research site within China had been typical or unusual, but most of the other advantages of the combination would be lost.

unimportant because of the possibility of doing research within China. If the situation within China were to continue to change in ways that would make the research environment more ideal and secure, then perhaps the need for Hong Kong interviewing would disappear. For the foreseeable future, however, the limitations and constraints involved in research within China will continue to make Hong Kong research a vital enterprise, either by itself or as part of the preparation for a research stay within China.

Part 2

Views from the Field

4. The New Face of Rural China: Kaixiangong Revisited after Half a Century

Kaixiangong is near my family's native place, a village in the same district where my own home town is located. I first undertook research there in 1936, before leaving for London for graduate studies in anthropology. When I graduated from Qinghua University in Peking in 1935, there was a regulation that permitted students who had conducted their studies well to go abroad for further training. But my teacher told me that if I wanted to go abroad for advanced studies, I should first carry out my own investigation so I could take my research materials with me. I first went to the Yao mountains in Guangxi province to study the Yao national minorities. But while traveling in the Yao mountains, I lost my way and injured myself when I fell into a tiger trap. So in 1936, I returned to my native district to rest and recover from my injuries.

At that time, my elder sister, who had been educated in Japan, was helping the peasants of the village to introduce modern, scientific methods of sericulture in Kaixiangong and to organize a collective silk reeling factory there. Introducing scientific knowledge into China's villages, I thought, was the proper direction for our country to take. If rural villages were to overcome the economic crisis facing them at that time, the peasants had to have proper technological skills, and scientific techniques had to be used to increase agricultural sideline production. Because of this conviction, I spent a month in Kaixiangong carrying out sociological research. My doctoral dissertation was based on this survey and published in English in 1939 under the title, Peasant Life in China.[1]

In May 1955, W.R. Geddes of the University of Sydney, Australia, visited Kaixiangong for a short period of five

---

1. Hsiao-tung Fei, Peasant Life in China (London: Routledge and Kegan Paul, 1939).

days, subsequently publishing the data he gathered in a monograph entitled, <u>Peasant Life in Communist China</u>.[2] And in 1957, I revisited Kaixiangong for twenty days. While[*] only part of my report of that visit was published, efforts are now being made to retrieve the research data, and I am hopeful that the materials were not seriously damaged in the years of turmoil following 1957.

I returned to Kaixiangong in October 1981 and again in January 1982, together with my still healthy and active elder sister, now 78 years old, who had made the first visit possible. These visits, I must confess, were more reunions with relatives and village elders than scientific field surveys. My reception in the village was warm beyond description. One of the young women who appeared in a photograph in my original book is now 78 years old. She came to visit me three times when I was there in October, having to walk an hour round-trip each time. The little children who had peeped through the windows to get a glimpse of me during my 1957 visit are now among the able leaders of the village's two production brigades. I have not quite recovered from the overwhelming expressions of friendship accorded me by these village peasants.

Despite the years of turmoil faced by Kaixiangong, I discovered during my recent visits that most of the basic data concerning its social conditions have been preserved intact. Therefore, the empirical data are available for analytic treatment of a period covering almost half a century. Moreover, the Chinese Academy of Social Sciences has decided to establish a permanent field research station at Kaixiangong, to be organized by the Academy's Institute of Sociology. We shall thus be able to continue adding to our body of historical knowledge about Kaixiangong and to trace its development for many years to come.

The enormous changes that China has experienced during this period of nearly half a century are unprecedented in world history—changes which have transformed a country under semi-colonial, semi-feudal rule into a socialist society. This transformation has affected every individual and every village in China. While Kaixiangong's experiences were

2. W.R. Geddes, <u>Peasant Life in Communist China</u> (Lexington, Kentucky: Society for Applied Anthropology Monograph No. 6, 1963).
* Editor's note: see Fei Hsiao-t'ung, "A Few Words on Sociology," in James P. McGough, editor and translator, <u>Fei Hsiao-t'ung: Dilemma of a Chinese Intellectual</u> (White Plains, N.Y.: M.E. Sharpe, 1979), pp. 32-39, for a translation of what was published.

basically the same as those of many other villages in China,
and while the village shares some common features with
millions of other Chinese villages, it also possesses
characteristics that are entirely unique and which
distinguish Kaixiangong from all other villages. Some of
these unique features—regional climate, for instance—reflect certain natural conditions which will persist. But
other features reflect the particular position or stage of
development of the Kaixiangong community. Let us have a
closer look then, at Kaixiangong—at the many changes that
have occurred over the past nearly half century, at the ups
and downs of those changes, at the current problems faced by
the villagers, and at the peasants' dreams and hopes for the
future.

Kaixiangong in Historical Perspective

Situated on the southeast bank of Lake Tai, the village
of Kaixiangong enjoys easy access to both Suzhou and
Hangzhou, two of the leading urban centers in the Lower
Yangtze region. As suggested by the popular Chinese saying,
"Suzhou and Hangzhou, paradise under heaven," the region's
advantageous economic conditions are reflected not only in
the higher productivity of agriculture, but also in the
advanced development of sideline occupations and village
industries, which are based on agricultural products. But
despite the advanced economic status the region has enjoyed
historically, the vicissitudes of Kaixiangong over the past
half century have sometimes been at odds with its objectively
advantageous conditions.

Kaixiangong in Decline: 1936-1949

In 1936, I concluded that the real issue in China was
the "hunger of the people." If my observation was correct at
the time I made that suggestion, the situation worsened
greatly, beginning not long after my first visit. In 1937,
shortly after I had completed my fieldwork, Kaixiangong was
occupied by the Japanese, and the cooperative silk filature
enterprise my sister had assisted in forming was
demolished—razed to the ground. From 1936 to 1949,
conditions continued to worsen. By the late 1940's,
landlords owned 56.6% of the farm land in the village, and
75% of the peasant households obtained their incomes from a
combination of working on rented land and from loan sharks.
Most of the peasants, therefore, lived on borrowed money.
Usually, they sold their food grain immediately after each
harvest to clear their debts and then again had to borrow
money to buy food. Their economic misery during this 13 year
period was exacerbated by repeated floods around the Lake Tai

region—a result of official inattention to water conservancy programs. Many peasants fled the village.

Under these circumstances, farm production remained stagnant between 1936 and 1949. In 1936, according to my figures, the output of rice was somewhat more than 300 catties per mu. Stagnation in agricultural output was compounded by oppressive taxation and rampant banditry. The miserable economic condition of Kaixiangong's peasants was the product of an exploitative system of land tenure and of the political power which sustained that system. Chinese peasants did not become masters of their own land until after 1949. Liberation in that year transformed the nature of political power in China; and the land reform of 1952 fundamentally transformed the system of rural economic production. With these two changes, one political, the other economic, China entered a new era.

Land Reform, Collectivization, and the Communes: 1949 - 1958

The economic effects of land reform may be brought into bold relief by comparing production figures for 1949 and 1952. The production of food grains which stagnated at 300 catties per mu from 1936 to 1949 had, according to the Geddes survey, reached 500 catties per mu in 1952. When Geddes conducted his investigation in 1955, the village had already entered the phase of agricultural cooperatives, and grain productivity had been further raised to 560 catties per mu.

The establishment of communes in 1958 appears, in retrospect, to have been premature. There is no need here to elaborate on the detrimental effects of ultra-leftist ventures during the years following 1959 -- an abundant literature on the subject is available in Western languages. Instead, I would like to highlight the beneficial effects of policy changes from 1962 to 1966, when the tendency toward ultra-leftism was rectified.

The Reforms of 1962-1966

During this period, the production brigade, rather than the much larger commune, became the basic accounting unit, and the principle of distributing income according to labor performed was officially adopted. This period also witnessed an increase in investments for basic improvements in farm land and irrigation systems, including electric-powered pumping facilities. As a result, grain production in

Kaixiangong increased at an annual rate of 8.25% from 1962 to 1966. Sericulture and silk reeling, which had a long tradition in Kaixiangong, were not only restored but also expanded. By 1966, villagers enjoyed an average per capita annual income of 119 yuan. The reintroduction of collective silkworm cultivation contributed to that increase. At that time, the ratio of income derived from collective agricultural production to that from agricultural sideline production, such as sericulture, was approximately 88:12.

Many commune members refer to 1962 as the turning point in their economic fortunes. "From that year on," they told me, "we enjoyed three meals of steamed rice a day." By three meals of steamed rice, they meant two catties of food grain for each able-bodied peasant.

The Cultural Revolution

But the period of rectification from 1962 to 1966 was followed by the Cultural Revolution. Although the rural sector of China's economy did not suffer so much as the urban sector during the period from 1966 to 1976, general stagnation prevailed in Kaixiangong and in other rural Chinese villages. Production incentives were drastically reduced by several policies and developments—the policy of promoting grain production at the expense of sideline occupations and rural industries; the increased power of higher level cadres unacquainted with local conditions, who often exercised arbitrary bureaucratic control; and the ultra-leftist emphasis on the doctrine of absolute egalitarianism. As a consequence, the rate of increase in grain production declined from the 8.25% of 1966 to 3.95% by 1976. Even those small increases were offset by increases in the population of Kaixiangong. During that 10 year period, commune members' average income hovered around 114 yuan, a slight decrease from the 1966 level.

Policy since 1978

Major policy changes introduced in 1978 finally removed the various negative effects of the leftist phase. Since then, economic development in rural communities such as Kaixiangong has entered a new and promising phase. By 1980, villagers were able to receive 1,000 catties of grain per year compared to 730 catties in 1962. Today, Kaixiangong has not only solved the problem of hunger, but peasants also have sufficient surplus grain to raise pigs and chickens as sideline occupations, thereby further increasing their household incomes.

How did Kaixiangong solve the problem of hunger? Let me answer that question by first viewing Kaixiangong in the larger economic context of other Chinese villages, and then within the context of the Lower Yangtze region where Kaixiangong is located.

A 1979 national survey of 700,000 production brigades revealed that no more than 1,632 brigades had per capita incomes in excess of 300 yuan. Only 71 production brigades had per capita incomes of 500 yuan or more. While the highest average per capita income reported by any brigade was 1,055 yuan, the national average was only 100 yuan. These findings enable us to appreciate the economic advantages of Kaixiangong.

The village of Kaixiangong, which consists today of two production brigades, has a per capita income of 300 yuan. Relative to the national scale, this places Kaixiangong in a "high-middle" position. But relative to the well-off region of Suzhou, of which Kaixiangong is a part, Kaixiangong is regarded as rather poor--well below average. This special position of Kaixiangong--a relatively poor village in one of the richest regions of China--allows us first, to compare Kaixiangong with other brigades of higher and lower income; second, to highlight differences in the economic transformation of China's rural villages; and third, to begin making some recommendations for further development in the Chinese countryside.

Sources of Peasant Income

Income in rural China is earned either from individual, private production or through participation in the collective economy. Moreover, income is derived either from the production of agricultural foodstuffs, from sideline production related to agriculture (such as raising silkworms), or from industrial production. In Kaixiangong, the production of agricultural foodstuffs, rather than agricultural sideline or industrial production, has been the dominant mode of production since 1936, when Japanese invaders demolished the village's silk filiatures. Even with the reintroduction of a collective silk industry in 1966, close to 90% of peasant income continued to come from agriculture.

Indeed, since 1978, the agricultural sector of Kaixiangong's collective economy has expanded, not in terms of its contribution to peasant income, but in terms of absolute output. Two factors are primarily responsible for this increase. First, the tendency toward egalitarianism which characterized both the period following the establishment of communes in 1958 and the ultra-leftist period of the Cultural Revolution, has ended. Now, rather than equal payment regardless of work performed in collective agricultural production, peasants are paid on the basis of the actual work they do, and their enthusiasm for participation in collective agricultural production has commensurately increased. Second, in an attempt to foster better management in agricultural production and to implement the principle of compensation according to work, Kaixiangong has introduced a new system of production responsibility. Land remains collectively owned, but individuals or households assume major responsiblity for certain tracts of that land. Because this type of responsibility system fosters material incentives to work, collective agricultural production in Kaixiangong has increased. Between 1978 and 1979, for example, collective grain production increased by 39.2%, and per mu output now stands at close to 2,000 catties.

But an even more important reason for the increase in peasant income in Kaixiangong since 1978 is the shift away from a single-minded concentration on food crop cultivation to the revival of subsidiary agricultural production, a revival that has taken place both within the collective economy and at the level of individual households. On the one hand, the private cultivation of cocoons has been absorbed into the collectively-owned silk industry. On the other hand, peasants are being encouraged to engage in a variety of household sideline occupations. Let us first look at the benefits to the peasants of individual household occupations.

Individual Household Occupations

During my 1936 visit to Kaixiangong, peasants were raising sheep as a household sideline activity, and they were raising rabbits when I returned in 1957. But at that time there was a tendency to neglect private sideline occupations. By 1981, however, sideline occupations had once again become extremely popular. It is not uncommon now for a peasant household to raise five, six, or even ten rabbits. The average per capita income from all sideline occupations reached 120-150 yuan in 1980, amounting to about half of all per capita income, and accounting as well for a major portion of the increases in per capita income from 1978 to 1981.

For instance, one of the households I visited during my recent trip consisted of three peasants. They were able to earn 1,087 yuan in 1980 by selling nine pigs, two sheep, and eight rabbits, by providing fertilizer from these animals to the collective, and by marketing the produce from their private plot. In addition, they received 660 yuan from their work in collective agriculture and agricultural sideline production. Thus, the household's total annual income was 1,747 yuan, an average of 549.7 yuan per household member. Another household of five, including four peasant laborers, earned a total income of 2,429 yuan in 1980, an average of 580.6 yuan per laborer. Since the family's total living expenses were only 960 yuan, their savings for the year amounted to 1,469 yuan. While income in these two households is higher than average in Kaixiangong, they are not considered particularly wealthy by village standards.

Collective Sideline Agricultural Production

In recent years, Kaixiangong has also witnessed an increase in collective sideline agricultural production, through both the collective raising of pigs and poultry and the renewal of silkworm production. Collective income from these sideline enterprises has increased, and with it, individual income. But Kaixiangong's success in increasing agricultural production must be seen within the broader context of China's population. In contrast to other Chinese communities, Kaixiangong can boast a two-fold success. It has increased its agricultural and agricultural sideline production and it has also limited its population increase.

Agricultural Production and Population Control

Rapid increase of population has a direct impact upon the average share of food available to individuals. In China, despite the great increase in agricultural production since Liberation, the average share of food grain available per person has not significantly increased. Between 1949 and 1978, despite a 162% increase in agricultural output, food grain available per person increased only 52%. As late as 1980, that is after the recent economic recovery began, the average share of foodgrain per person (excluding soybeans and tubers) remained at 580 catties a year (or 1.5 catties per day). Since this is the average figure for China, it is apparent that some of China's more economically underdeveloped areas, unlike Kaixiangong, have yet to solve the problem of hunger.

Let us consider another aspect of the relationship between population and hunger. In 1917, China's total population was 440 million. Despite the wars and famines of

the intervening years, China's population reached 540 million
by 1949. Concomitant with the economic growth of the 1950's,
100 million people were added to the Chinese population
during the first eight years of the People's Republic and
another 100 million during the following nine years. By
1971, the total population reached 840 million, and the 1980
estimate was around one billion. The rate of increase during
the 31 years from 1950 to the end of 1980 was 81%, an annual
increase of 1.9%.

Because the negative effect of rapid population increase
on economic growth was not fully appreciated in China in the
early 1950's, and because the slogans encouraging birth
control in 1956 were not supported with vigorous
administrative measures, the population continued to increase
after 1950, with two "peak periods"—one in 1954-1957 (with
an annual rate of 2.4%) and one in 1962-1970 (with a rate of
2.54%). The 1963 rate, reflecting recovery from the "three
bad years" of 1959, 1960, and 1961 following the formation of
communes, was as high as 3.35%. It was not until 1970, when
coordinated birth control programs were seriously
implemented, that the rate of population increase began a
steady decline. The sharp drop to only 1.27% in 1976, a
phenomenon rare in world demographic history, helped reduce
the annual increase for the 10 year period of 1970-1980 to
1.84%, a rate below the 1.97% rate of world population growth
during the same period. After 1976, however, the decline of
population growth slowed, as those born during the 1954-1957
"peak period" reached their childbearing years. The net
population increase since 1976 has been 11 million per year.

Another important demographic characteristic of China is
the uneven distribution of the population. Over 90% of
China's people are concentrated in the southeastern half of
the country, where population density is ten times that of
northwestern China. Within southeastern China, economically
advanced regions such as the Lower Yangtze valley and the
Pearl River Delta are among the most densely populated areas
of the world, with 400 to 500 persons per square kilometer.

Kaixiangong is located in one of those densely populated
areas. In 1936, its total population was 1,458, and in 1955,
when Geddes studied the village, it was 1,440. The slight
decline in population during that period may be attributed
not only to the effects of war and the tradition of
infanticide as a means of birth control, but also to a shift
in village boundaries. More recent figures indicate that the
population of Kaixiangong had reached 1,889 by 1966 and was
2,308 in 1981—a 32.5% and 61% increase respectively over
1955.

While population growth in Kaixiangong seems high, it was nonetheless slower than the national rate for the same period. This achievement is even more impressive in light of indications that mortality has also declined. Although I have no hard facts to back up my impression of declining mortality, there is some indirect evidence to that effect. During my 1981 visit, official records indicated that there were 117 senior citizens, or 5% of the total population at or above age 70. During 1936, there were only 17 such people—1% of the population.

Kaixiangong has long been conscious of and sensitive to the problems of population. In the past, that awareness encouraged such countermeasures as abortion and infanticide. Today, therefore, the scientifically planned birth control programs are understandably welcomed by villagers. Local cadres assured me that, "we have no difficulties in carrying out the birth control program here," and their assertion is supported by figures indicating a general decline in the rate of population increase since 1977 (and even a minus figure for one year).

The experience of Kaixiangong indicates the importance of public support for the birth control program. In terms of the relationship between population and food, Kaixiangong is indeed in a better position than many other rural communities. Rational use of comparatively rich soil has enabled the village to increase agricultural production. With relatively slow population growth, the fruits of increased agricultural production can be more fully enjoyed by the villagers. While the average amount of foodgrain available yearly throughout China is 580 catties per capita, the figure stands at 1,000 catties in Kaixiangong. Thus, from this small window—Kaixiangong—we can see why population control is so essential to the solution of China's lingering problem of hunger—not to mention the possible rewards family planning may provide in terms of expanding and improving opportunities for education and employment. According to even the most conservative estimates, the population of China is likely to reach 1.2 billion by the end of this century. Most of that population will remain in rural areas. This is a basic fact, from which our theories of Chinese economy and society must begin and from which our policies promoting development must be derived.

Alongside the successful development of collectively organized agriculture and agricultural sideline production stand cruel and inescapable facts. Not only is the price of grain low, restricting potential income from the production of basic foodstuffs, but in many parts of China, including

Kaixiangong, the limits of agricultural growth using current farming techniques have been, or are about to be, reached. Moreover, factors that limit further increases in grain production also negatively affect those sideline activities, such as pig and poultry raising and cultivating silkworms, which depend on agricultural products. Pigs and poultry depend on food grain, and silkworms require mulberry leaves. The restoration of sericulture in Kaixiangong was made possible by new electric pumping facilities, which transformed a large tract of flooded area into mulberry groves. But the prospect for further increases in mulberry acreage in Kaixiangong appears as bleak as that for further increases in the output of grain.

It is within this context then, within the context of the approaching limits both of agricultural growth and of expanding sideline occupations that depend on agricultural products, that the new promise of collectively organized rural industry must be understood.

The Promise of Rural Industries

During my earliest fieldwork in Kaixiangong in 1936, I became convinced that in rural areas where population pressures limited the expansion of arable land, village industries were an important means to raise the peasant standard of living. I discussed the relationship between agriculture, household sideline production, and collectively owned industries in Peasant Life in China. After my return from London, I acquired a firmer grasp of the problem in the course of field surveys conducted in Yunnan province. The results of these studies appeared in Earthbound China.[3] During my visit to Kaixiangong in 1957, I expressed concern about the lack of official support for the restoration of village industries. Some of my views have been validated recently, and it is still my opinion that village industries remain a key to the solution of China's rural economic problems.

In a highly populated country such as China, once the problem of basic subsistence has been solved, the next attack on rural poverty must involve what I have called "spreading industry to the countryside"--the proliferation of a great variety of small scale industries throughout the countryside rather than the concentration of a small number of large industries in big cities. This "spreading industries to the

---

3. Hsiao-tung Fei and Chih-I Chang, Earthbound China: A Study of Rural Economy in Yunnan (London: Routledge and Kegan Paul, 1948).

countryside" is a recent development in Kaixiangong and is a major factor in the increase of peasant income. Several new collectively owned industries were introduced in 1979, including two soybean mills, one silk reeling filiature, and one silk weaving workshop. As a result, while all three sectors of the collective economy—agriculture, agricultural sideline production, and industry—have registered increases in output, the proportion of peasant income derived from the collective agricultural sector has declined in proportion to that derived from agricultural sideline production and industry. To take one of Kaixiangong's production brigades as an example, in 1979, the proportion of collective income derived from agriculture, agricultural sideline production, and rural industries was 50.3%, 22.6%, and 26.6% respectively. By 1980, with the introduction of new collective industries, these proportions had undergone considerable alteration—41% came from agriculture, 19% from agricultural sideline production, and 40% from collective industries.

What is happening today in Kaixiangong as it introduces collective industry is also happening in many other parts of China. Many formerly impoverished production brigades are breaking out of the cycle of poverty through the introduction of sideline enterprises and rural industries. In the Suzhou district where Kaixiangong is located, my investigations revealed that in those brigades that relied only on agricultural production for collective income, the average per capita income of peasants only rarely passed the barrier of 100 yuan a year. In those areas that had added agricultural sideline production to their collective endeavor, per capita peasant income could only be increased to between 200 and 300 yuan a year. But those brigades that had developed collective industries were able to make major breakthroughs. Some of these brigades have already achieved average per capita incomes surpassing 500 yuan per year.

This is not to say that the development of rural industries is without problems. Many brigades are without certain sources of raw materials and fuel, and the market for some of the products of rural industries is not always constant. Moreover, many brigade cadres lack experience in industrial management and commercial trading.

Solving many of these problems depends on education. Due to the 10 year turmoil of the Cultural Revolution, the educational level of most village cadres is not very high. Most have only a primary school education. In Kaixiangong, with a population of 550 households, there is not a single university student. There is a saying among peasants, "to leave middle school is not as good as not going to middle school at all," reflecting their view that education is useless because it is not practical. It is useless because it is divorced from production. This is a powerful indictment against those of us engaged in education. The basis of modernization is scientific knowledge, and the villages, in order to modernize, must have modern, practical knowledge. The separation of academic and practical training is a question we educators must ponder deeply. In the 1920's, my sister took the scientific and technical knowledge that she had acquired to the countryside. Why can this not be so today? We intellectuals must look beneath the surface, face reality, face the masses.

The question today is not whether we want to develop brigade industries, but rather how to build brigade industries and to channel them along the socialist path. This is a new task in our country's path towards modernization, but if we carry out proper and thorough investigations, we can work together with the masses to solve this problem. The introduction and development of rural industry not only helps impoverished brigades break out of the cycle of poverty, it also has the effect of increasing the ratio of industrial labor in the national economy and of avoiding an excessive concentration of laborers divorced from agricultural production. Introduction of rural industry reduces the gap between workers and peasants. What I found in Kaixiangong, therefore, was particularly exciting. A dream of many years is now emerging as reality. I was witnessing the beginning of a new course in Chinese rural development.

New Hopes

With the problems of hunger and clothing solved, as they have been in Kaixiangong, and with many peasants now able to save substantial sums of money, one must wonder what new demands have been created by the new economic situation. How will peasants spend their newly acquired savings? What are the hopes of the peasants for the future?

My own observations suggest that the major new concern of Kaixiangong villagers is housing and furniture. The housing problem is indeed serious. Most of the villagers are living today in the same houses in which they lived in 1936, and those houses now appear more dilapidated than before. But they are providing shelter for a much larger number of people. In one production brigade, I discovered that over ten families lived inside three household gates which, in

1936, contained only three families. According to housing statistics provided by village cadres, living space available per person increased by only .04 rooms between 1948 and 1980. Since each room is about twenty square meters, the increase amounts to less than one square meter per person.

Today, major expenditures for housing and housing improvement are usually made on the occasion of marriage. In the past, with meager savings and a major housing shortage, peasant households were faced with the alternative of either postponing marriage or dividing limited living quarters into still smaller apartments to accommodate new conjugal units. With the increased savings made possible in recent years, however, most families with sons of marriageable age are busy with housing projects. In the past year, fifty new houses have been added to the cluster of 250 households along the southern bank of Kaixiangong village. Most of the new structures are additions or extensions to existing houses, and the new construction adds some confusion to the already chaotic layout of the housing settlement.

The occasion of a village wedding is not only an opportunity to build or modify housing, it is also the occasion to add new pieces of furniture, such as beds, tables, and chairs. New furniture is acquired during the process of wedding negotiations, a process which usually occupies the full attention of the parents of both sides during the period between engagement and wedding. In Kaixiangong, it is largely the groom's responsiblity to provide the living quarters for his new bride, while the bride's side is responsible for furnishing those quarters. The li-jin, or "honorarium," which the groom gives the bride is actually a sort of stipend to underwrite the cost of furniture, bedding, and clothing; but the value of items in the bride's dowry usually far exceeds the value of the groom's li-jin payment. In short, the responsibility for furnishing the newlyweds' living quarters is shared.

The most extravagant part of the marriage expense, however, is the elaborate and costly wedding banquet provided for relatives and friends. While these feasts serve to give social sanction to the new marriage, and therefore serve a useful sociological function, from an economic viewpoint, they are wasteful and expensive.

Such an extravagant expenditure of funds on marriage feasts highlights a major problem that has resulted from recent economic advances in rural China. Many rural households now hold substantial surplus reserves of cash. Because sufficient supplies of manufactured consumer goods have yet to be made available to the countryside, peasants are forced either to save or to spend their money on such fleeting luxuries as wedding banquets. The new problem must eventually be solved through the supply of more commodities to the countryside.

Conclusion

Rural China today is embarking on a new and promising path of development. As Chinese peasants march along that path, they will face a number of problems, problems which China's intellectuals can help to solve. The peasants need education—education of a practical type that will help them to grapple with the problems they face in their daily work. They need science and management skills in order to give full play to the benefits of a socialist economy. The task of the social anthropologists and sociologists is to understand those problems in order to assist the peasants in their march toward modernization. We need to carry out more investigations of rural China, to conduct the type of "micro-sociological" studies that were advocated by scholars in the 1930's. My own re-study of Kaixiangong has just begun. With the establishment of a permanent field research station there, I and my colleagues at the Chinese Academy of Social Sciences now have the opportunity to continue our investigation and to assist the peasants in solving their problems. In time, such investigations will be expanded to other rural areas of China as well, and with them, "people's sociology" will also develop.

5. Field Research in China's Communes: Views of a "Guest"

Successful field research in China is possible. This is abundantly clear from the experiences of several social scientists, myself included, who have recently returned from the first wave of exchanges with the People's Republic. But all research takes place under the watchful eyes of research or educational organizations that sponsor visas, and in the field access to data is strictly controlled by local administrative offices, some of which are specially set up to deal with foreigners. I will discuss my own research experience here and then discuss some implications that it may have for future research in China, exploring the extent to which administrative control over research processes limits or enhances the scope of opportunities.

My research was designed to assess the impact that economic development has had on local administrative structures in the countryside. I wanted to examine how commune organization has adapted to a changing economic and political environment. I also wanted to gather extensive data to address a number of more narrow problems. Why is it that some villages develop more quickly than others? How successful have the Chinese been in suppressing income differentials within villages and production teams, China's units of collective farming composed of 30 to 40 families? Does the degree of equality or inequality vary among villages? Why?

My plan was to gather extensive standardized data on all production and administrative units of a single commune, to conduct household surveys in a selected sample of teams, and finally to interview at length officials at all levels of the commune, in all departments. In order to do this, I proposed

An earlier version of this chapter appears in <u>Studies in</u> ← <u>Comparative International Development</u>, Volume XVIII.

and was able to live in a more or less ordinary Chinese commune in Hebei Province for six months, engaged in full time research.

On the American side, the research was sponsored, negotiated, and funded by the Committee on Scholarly Communication with the People's Republic of China—the organization described in the introduction, which is responsible for facilitating research by Americans in China under the national level bilateral exchanges. On the Chinese side, I was affiliated with the Institute of Agricultural Economics under the Chinese Academy of Social Sciences. The Academy sponsored my visa and made initial arrangements for the research, but once I left Peking, I was entirely in the hands of provincial and local authorities who made all the concrete arrangements and controlled access to people and data. Before describing my experience in more detail and outlining the implications of my research for other social scientists planning research in China, I should say that the research was highly successful from my point of view. My Chinese hosts went to extraordinary lengths to insure that the objectives outlined in my research proposal were achieved, and I am extremely grateful to them.

Floating a Research Proposal into the Field

American social scientists are fully accustomed to running their research proposals through the gauntlet of funding committees, which attempt to enforce high academic standards for the projects they back. But for those contemplating field research in China, as other contributors to this volume also recognize, several more gates must be passed before research can be carried out. First, a proposal must be approved by a Chinese research or educational organization, and second, a proposal must be acceptable to regular administrative cadres who are responsible for the territory or organization in which a researcher works.

In my case, I am a political scientist and had previously conducted research from the outside, both in the United States and in Hong Kong, on China's rural administrative system. Realizing that the Chinese had no academic research organization conducting local level political studies, and that such a topic might be too politically sensitive anyway, I intentionally framed my research topic so that it would be of interest to agricultural economists. I aimed my study at the system of administering agricultural development, and I made a conscious effort to put the proposal in terms which were politically neutral in the Chinese context, yet seemed generally sympathetic to China's overall goals of agricultural modernization. I did not, however, "gut" the proposal. I made it clear that in order to achieve my research goals, I would need to collect systematic economic and administrative data and would need to interview, somehow, household heads.

Before my trip to China, I had regarded the writing of a research proposal as an intellectual exercise to clarify research plans and also as a means to secure funding. But the Chinese, when agreeing to sponsor a particular project, tend to view a proposal more like a contract, as Burton Pasternak also emphasizes. Thus it was fortunate that I had defined my topic clearly enough that the Chinese knew what to expect. When I arrived in Peking, I read a Chinese translation of my proposal that had been prepared by the Institute of Agricultural Economics and knew immediately that there was little if any misunderstanding about what I would do.

[margin note: proposal as contract]

The Academy had circulated my proposal to officials in the Hebei Province Foreign Affairs Office who proceeded to select a commune that had the characteristics I had requested, namely, that the commune be in a Mandarin-speaking region, that it not be a model commune or a surburban vegetable-growing commune, that it be more or less average in size and wealth, but also that it be a commune that had experienced growth in the output of food grains over the past ten years. The province handed the matter to the Shijiazhuang Prefectural Foreign Affairs Office, the Prefecture to the Huailu County Office, and, finally, the County selected Dahe Commune, which fit my research needs perfectly. Dahe, it turned out, is more or less average economically for the region in which it is located, while the region is somewhat above average for China as a whole.

[margin note: general requirements]

The lesson I would draw for future proposal writers is that proposals should be crystal clear about what is absolutely necessary for successful research. It is especially important that research proposals communicate goals in non-technical language so that ordinary, literate, administrative cadres can grasp the essentials of the research. At the same time, a proposal should give the Chinese as much flexibility as possible to set up a situation that satisfies research needs. If all requests are overly specific, there is a risk of inadvertently putting the administrators who arrange for the particulars of a project into a corner. Judging by my experience, these

[margin note: clarity of proposal]

administrators are not likely to try to subvert the
intentions of a project by, for example, sending a field
researcher to a highly atypical area that might restrict the
general applicability of findings. Viewing the proposal like
a contract, the Chinese also feel the need to hold up their
end of the bargain. This is especially true for local-level
administrators who tend to treat the proposal as they would
any administrative directive coming from the central
government. That is, it becomes their duty to carry it out to
the fullest, as they clearly did in my case.

Field researchers should also expect that local
administrators, as well as Academy officials, will not be
receptive either to expanding the scope of research or to
adding new methods for collecting data beyond what is already
specified or implied in the proposal. This was communicated
to me in a fairly unsubtle way after I began my research and
tried to test the limits of what I could do. Thus,
everything that a researcher wants to do must be in the
proposal from the start.

This restriction, however, presents a problem to the
proposal writer. We don't know the limits yet on what topics
or research methods can be pursued. Should a proposal be
written conservatively to assure that the Chinese will accept
it, or should a potentially sensitive method be placed in the
proposal, risking rejection by the Chinese? In my case, I
had decided not to include plans for administering a
questionnaire to local cadres designed to elicit subjective
attitudes toward difficulties involved in their
administrative duties. In retrospect, I am sorry that I did
not include it while making clear that if the method proved
unacceptable to the Chinese, it would not seriously affect
the value of my study. Tentative parts of proposals might be
surrounded by language such as "if it is convenient...," or
"if it does not cause problems, I would like to..." If the
rest of the research proposal is written well enough that the
Chinese clearly understand the goals of the research and the
methods necessary to reach those goals, they will be in a
position to evaluate part of a proposal that may be less
crucial. Nonetheless, any tentative parts of a proposal must
be clearly related to the central research goals, or the
proposition will have no validity from the Chinese viewpoint.
In fact, any request, both in the proposal or later on the
ground, whether it be about where to live or what method of
transportation to use, should be rationalized in terms of its
relationship to the overall research goals that are in the
proposal. Thus, the proposal turns out to be an extremely
important document throughout the research period.

In the Field

Although I was accompanied to the field by a junior researcher from the Institute of Agricultural Economics who helped in explaining my research needs to local cadres, and who in essence assumed political responsiblity for how to interpret my proposal, once in the provinces, he was nearly as much of an outsider as I was. I was a guest of the province, the prefecture, the county, the commune, and any village or household that I visited. My hosts played their roles well by taking very good care of me, and I would have been a bad guest had I rejected the elaborate, and sometimes slightly absurd, arrangements that had been made for me. From the start there was never any real possibility that I could become a detached, impartial observer, in full control of what was happening to me or of the data that I collected.

Although my hosts in the localities had some grasp of the problem I was studying, they had little knowledge of or any real sympathy with the goals of social science research. When I finally arrived at the commune, I had accumulated an entourage of five persons, including the researcher from the Institute. The Provincial and Prefectural Foreign Affairs Offices each sent an interpreter, who were basically superfluous since I speak Chinese, and the Prefectural Foreign Affairs Office sent a higher ranking official who had been responsible for making arrangements on the site. The foreign affairs officials are responsible for ferrying foreigners in and out of the labyrinth of highly segmented work and residential units that make up Chinese society, and their main professional charge seems to be to make the foreigners comfortable and, as they say, "to promote friendship between the Chinese and American people." They do this mainly by arranging things so that foreigners do not have to lift a finger. For these persons, my visit to China was simply one more professional assignment, although the length and nature of my stay were new to them.

But for the commune and county officials, I was the first foreign visitor they had ever entertained. I still can't say for certain just why the commune agreed to take me, or whether they had any choice in the matter. The commune cadres went to a great deal of trouble for me. They walled off and refurbished a row of offices in the main village where I lived with my entourage, a cook, and a custodian. If these elaborate arrangements would lead you to think that I might feel surrounded and excessively watched, you are right. My first few weeks in the village were extremely difficult personally, and my hosts would not even let me jog alone in the early morning for fear that "something might happen."

Everyone was, at first, clearly apprehensive both about what my intentions were and that they would unintentionally mistreat me. As time wore on I grew to understand and sympathize with these apprehensions more and more. My hosts knew full well that I would return home and write about what I saw, and they did not want to get a black eye from it. They did not want me to say that they had treated me badly, and they did not want me to say "unfair" things about China's political, social, or economic system that would reflect badly on them. The Chinese are still somewhat defensive about their socialist system, especially when it is assessed by foreigners who, they fear, may have unreasonable prejudices against it. Criticism is sincerely welcomed, but only in a constructive and friendly spirit. The Chinese don't mind if you tell them that women's roles are different from and unequal to those of men, but they don't like it if you fail to say that things have improved and people are trying to change for the better.

After a few weeks in the village, however, word circulated back to me that my hosts decided I was "friendly" (as opposed to hostile). People began to relax more, and some of the people from the province and prefecture were withdrawn. I became personally very friendly with some of the local cadres, and living and working in the village became more pleasant and productive all the time. There are two lessons to be drawn from this, which I will develop in a moment. First, it takes time to develop a rapport with people who have control over the data needed for research. Second, it is crucially important that a researcher in fact be "friendly," that he make a real effort to be as little of a burden as possible and to reinforce and help the people on whom he relies.

But even though suspicions about me eased over time and people became genuinely friendly, I was never able to take personal charge and directly arrange all of my research activities, as I had been accustomed to in the past. The day after I arrived in the commune, I sat down with my hosts and they asked me for a complete schedule of research activities for the next six months. They wanted me to tell them how much time I needed for each phase of the research project so that they could plan in advance, months in advance it seemed, all appointments or other activities. Their idea was that I would put forth all of my requests at one time, they would plan all of my activities at one time, and we could then proceed without delay according to plan. Although I did have a general sense of the organization of my work, I could not tell them how long each phase would take, and until I had a better sense of the mechanics of gathering data and of just

what I would be allowed to do, it would be difficult for me
to tell them very concretely just how to set up my
activities. For example, I wanted to get a lot of
statistical materials on production team economic activities,
but at the start I did not know exactly where records that
contained the kind of detailed statistics I needed were kept.
If such records were maintained at commune headquarters, my
research activities would be quite different than if they
were kept at the teams. As it turned out, my worst case
scenario came true, and I found that the records were
maintained by accountants who, if they left their posts and
were transferred elsewhere, took their books with them.

Nonetheless, their need to plan was real, and this is
something with which all field researchers will have to learn
to cope. Activities in administrative and productive units
are planned from top to bottom. Since I was hosted by the
commune level, all of my activities within the commune had to
be planned and arranged by commune cadres. I could not
simply contact cadres or ordinary commune members on my own
and set up appointments. Part of the reason for this is that
everyone was very busy with their own activities, all of
which were in some way administratively sanctioned. Whenever
I spent time interviewing or otherwise using someone's time,
they would not, obviously, be able to do what they ordinarily
would have done. They had to be released from their ordinary
activities, and this had to be planned, just as their
original activities had been planned. The need to rely on
others to arrange appointments probably sounds horrifying to
Western researchers, but it also has its advantages. I was
in fact able to talk with everyone with whom I asked to talk,
and did not have to become personally involved in all the
details of setting up appointments. And although I cringed
at the thought, it was also convenient for research purposes
that no one could actually refuse to see me. Initially, I
saw the system of planning as an encumbrance on my work, but
over time I came to view it differently. The fact was that
the entire administrative staff of the commune was at my
disposal to give me data or help me gather it, and this
greatly raised the efficiency of my research. The problem
was that my hosts arranged appointments so efficiently and
rapidly that it was difficult for me to keep up, and I
frequently had to request a day or two off in order to catch
up with typing my notes.

But the efficiency achieved in setting up appointments
did not always erase the frustration I felt at the total
inability to arrange my own time. I communicated my research
needs to persons assigned to the project. They in turn
comunicated my requests to the commune Vice-Party secretary

who had been assigned to coordinate my activities in the commune. Then they would all meet together with other relevant cadres to plan appointments. The whole process was kept hidden from me, and they rarely communicated to me any scheduling difficulties that arose. Not infrequently, these scheduling difficulties caused last minute reshuffling of appointments which, in a few instances, were not communicated to me until after I had gone out my door and mounted my bicycle, about to head out to one of the neighboring villages. My hosts expressed some bewilderment that I did not like being excluded from their decision-making about arranging my time, and occasionally I also wondered why I reacted with annoyance, which I kept well hidden, since I was in fact able to do virtually everything I requested. The reason, of course, is that it was a difficult personal adjustment to live for an extended period of time in a fish bowl, where I had absolutely no personal privacy or independence. These situations have provided many amusing anecdotes for short-term travelers in China, but it is quite something else to live and work under them for an extended period.

I tried to view my plight philosophically, and learned a great deal from the experience after I realized that inability to arrange my own time mirrored the situation in which most ordinary administrative cadres find themselves. I was told repeatedly that in China people follow their leaders. As long as they follow their leader, their leader will take care of them, and followers do not have to take responsiblity for what happens, or take any real initiative in solving problems. My Chinese friends found it difficult to imagine the American life that I described to them in which I did not have an organization to take care of me or tell me what to do. If I tried to hint that I was not always comfortable with arrangements that had been made for me, they just laughed and said that I probably did not understand how things worked in China. But I quickly did grasp the fact that I could not buck the system. I had been more or less absorbed into the administrative routines of the commune that I came to study and was expected to follow the rules just like everybody else. I too had to learn quickly how to follow the leader.

Gathering Data

But by following the leader, I was able to gather an immense and unique set of data that will be extremely valuable for analyzing China's rural development. The system really did not get in the way that much and on balance was more of a help than a hindrance. Most of my dissatisfaction with arrangements resulted from personal discomfort at feeling so restricted, and not from frustration over any inability to gather data that I felt were essential to my project. I used, basically, three different methods to collect data about the communes: interviews with local cadres; interviews with household heads; and statistical questionnaires given to brigades and teams in the commune.

I began initially by interviewing heads of commune departments, and heads of other organizations that operated within the commune, such as the Supply and Marketing Cooperative, the Grain Station, and the Tax Office. These organizations are administered directly by higher level cadres rather than by commune-level cadres. I was asked to provide a list of questions ahead of time, and the interviewees came with a prepared outline and spoke as if giving a lecture. However, I did frequently interrupt to ask follow-up questions on interesting points, and the interviews proceeded more or less as structured discussions. These interviews were fairly broad in scope. I asked interviewees to describe their work and that of their departments, and to provide statistics that could be used to describe the work of their departments over the past ten years. For example, I asked the credit cooperatives to give me figures for deposits and loans over a ten year period, and asked the Supply and Marketing Cooperative to give me ten years of sales turnover and profit figures. I also posed questions about typical problems encountered in the course of their work, many of which I knew about from my previous research in Hong Kong. The effectiveness of these interviews varied greatly with the personality of the interviewee. Interviewees varied in their ability to articulate, and some were clearly reticent to go much beyond the official line or to volunteer information that went beyond my questions. Many, however, provided interesting, in-depth descriptions of their work. In this respect problems of interviewing in China are similar to interviewing elsewhere. Obviously, some topics are best left undiscussed, such as corruption involving specific individuals. But in general, I felt local officials made a sincere effort to answer my questions in a forthright, complete manner and tried to give me an accurate picture of their work. One check I have on the reliability of these interviews is a comparison with data I gathered in Hong Kong from interviews with emigrees. In general, there is no great discrepancy between these two different sources.

The more my questions delved into concrete matters that my interviewees dealt with every day in their work, the better were their answers. For this reason, it is a real asset for anyone doing such research to have done previous interview work in Hong Kong, as Martin Whyte suggests here in his discussion of the comparative merits of research in China and research at its gate. Unless questions are phrased in the exact terminology that cadres themselves use to describe their administrative work, it is difficult to get a good response, and the efficiency of interview research is greatly reduced. This terminology is difficult to acquire through newspapers and textbooks, and even the interpreters assigned to the project did not know the proper translations for many terms, or even their precise meaning in Chinese, since they were not specialists in rural administration or agricultural economics.

One problem that occurred, especially at the beginning of my stay, was that as many as seven persons in addition to me and the interviewee attended the interviews. The large number of people made it more difficult to establish an informal atmosphere and put the interviewee at ease. Sometimes, when the interviewee's answer was not clear, or he appeared confused by a question, others present would answer. This was extremely unhelpful, because I wanted most of all to understand how local cadres understood their own work and the problems associated with it. When others from outside the commune tried to answer these questions, their answers tended to be abstract or a simple repetition of problems and examples often discussed in the People's Daily. Since I also read the People's Daily, I learned little from these responses. Later on, after I suggested that so many people were not really needed at the interviews, a suggestion which baffled my hosts, fewer people attended the interviews, and they went more smoothly.

Initially there was also a problem caused by the presence of interpreters. Both interpreters worked very hard to interpret the detailed interviews as accurately as possible, which strained their English to the limits. But basically I had no desire or need to have the interviews interpreted for me. Nonetheless, I felt very awkward asking them not to interpret since that was the responsibility assigned to them. Both interpreters were very sincere and hard working, and since they were not employed by me, I did not think it proper for me to tell them not to perform their assigned duties. My initial language problems stemmed principally from unfamiliarity with the local accent, a problem which, to a much lesser degree, also plagued the interpreters. What I really needed when I did not understand what was said was to hear an explanation in standard Mandarin. It would have been impossible for me to rely completely on interpreters and efficiently complete my work. Interpreting required more time and set up a barrier between me and the interviewee. In addition, it was extremely difficult to provide precise, accurate translations of many of the detailed discussions held. Many terms commonly used in the villages do not have precise equivalents in English. As time passed and my mastery of the local accent improved, it became increasingly obvious that the interpreters were impeding the interviews, and they more or less voluntarily stopped providing translations.

Although when I first arrived there were people surrounding me all the time, there was no one actually working for me. I found this a disadvantage, because it was awkward to ask any of these people to do anything for me. I asked that my hosts provide someone who could help me draft and administer questionnaires. They found an ideal person who had graduated from upper-middle school and had served as a brigade (village) Party secretary for over eight years. He knew the people and the workings of the commune inside and out, and was a tremendous asset in the research. His suggestions about how to gather data were uniformly practical, while those from persons outside the commune were often uninformed and not very helpful.

My assistant was crucial during the second phase of data gathering, when I administered a questionnaire to all ninety-six production teams and sixteen production brigades in the commune. With the help of my assistant, I drew up a questionnaire concerning production and administrative matters for all of these units. This turned out to be a huge project. I asked for a ten year run of figures, but it turned out that production teams do not keep their books in very good order. Teams rotate accountants frequently, and when an accountant goes, the books go with him. Thus, what should have been a relatively simple project ended up being a mammoth one, as accountants scurried all over trying to round up the books. This took some accountants as long as fifteen days.

We administered the forms first in one brigade as an experiment, where I realized that it would take the accountants a very long time to complete the forms. I knew that somehow the production units to which these accountants belonged would have to be reimbursed for their time. This is very clearly stipulated in China's own administrative rules, so I asked the commune to give me an estimate of how expensive it would be to have all forms completed by all units in the commune. If it proved too expensive, I planned to reduce the number of forms. The commune responded at that point, however, that I should not worry about the money involved since the figures I had asked for were important to

my research. They did not want to see the project fail
because I did not have enough funds. Eventually the commune
asked for, and I paid, 900 <u>yuan</u>. The amount, however, did
not come close to reimbursing the commune for actual
expenses, that is, the amount that it had to pay the teams
and brigades, which was probably two or three times the
amount I was asked to pay. My hosts were very generous with
me, I think, partly because the expenses encountered were
truly unanticipated, and my hosts wanted to make the first
round of academic exchanges a complete success. I would
expect that both sides will be better able to anticipate real
expenses in the future and that the Chinese will ask
researchers to pay in full for whatever costs they may incur.

After we administered the forms in our experimental
brigade, we revised some to make them easier to fill in, and
we reproduced them on a hand stencil machine -- a cheaper
alternative to having them printed in the nearby county seat.
I then bicycled personally to all brigades in the commune to
deliver the forms and explain how to complete them. I feel,
in retrospect, that this was an important gesture since the
task of filling them in turned out to be so difficult. When
we began delivering the forms, the commune vice-secretary
accompanied us to encourage the brigade accountants to devote
full attention to getting the forms filled in rapidly. This
measure of support from the commune, I believe, was also
important.

After the forms were delivered, the commune accountant
assumed principal responsibility for seeing that brigades
filled them in. At meetings of accountants which he convened
for training purposes, he helped solve problems encountered
in the course of filling out the forms. He also urged
brigade and team accountants to fill them in as rapidly as
possible. About two months later, he gave me the completed
forms.

At that point, my assistant and I carefully read all
forms to check that they were filled in properly. We
prepared a list of mistakes for each brigade and had several
meetings of brigade accountants to explain the remaining
problems. These were cleared up in another week and the
forms are now relatively complete. Some teams were, in the
end, unable to produce some of the statistics which I
requested, but this did not result from a lack of trying.
All in all I am struck by two things: the enormous effort and
continuous support which the commune administrative staff
gave in order to get the forms filled in, and the total
impossibility of completing any such project, even on a much
smaller scale, without local-level administrative support. I

now have in my files data on all units which include the following: detailed year-end balance sheets of income, expenses, savings, and distribution; lists of major capital assets for each year and the gross value of capital assets; planted area, yields, and disposition of output of major crops; accumulation and welfare fund income and expenditures; registered population, labor power, and labor utilization. I also have rates of leadership change in all of these units, simple biographical data on all current cadres at all levels of the commune, subjective assessments by commune leaders of the quality of leadership in each village, and assessments of the quality of land in each village. Analysis of this material should prove extremely interesting.

The final method of gathering data involved interviews with household heads. My assistant and I went to over 200 households to gather information about family and individual income, budgets, education, job histories, political activities, etc. My assistant accompanied me on all interviews and took notes on a chart that we developed to accommodate the information that we planned to record. In the beginning, the presence of my assistant was especially helpful until I had mastered the thick local accent, which tended to be much heavier with women. I interviewed family heads of almost all families in five different production teams, including the richest and the poorest in the commune. I could not interview all household heads, my hosts told me, because of illness, insanity, and absence. In cases where I could not personally visit a houshold, a cadre from the team or brigade would visit the house for me and fill in the forms, so that I now do have complete data on all households in the five teams. I do not believe that my hosts were trying to hide anything, because among families I did interview were former landlords and even a former Guomindang military policeman who had spent 12 years in a labor reform camp in Xinjiang. The data I gathered here will prove very useful for analyzing, among other things, patterns of income distribution in the countryside.

Some Preliminary Findings

Dahe Commune is probably representative of a broad spectrum of moderately prosperous grain-producing communes. In the past few years, its income has increased enough to push it into the highest quarter of income distribution in rural China. In earlier years it was probably closer to the median rural income. But its road to relative prosperity has not been an easy one.

Prior to the end of the Japanese occupation, a strong

Communist underground was already operating in the region, with at least one Party member in each village. When Communist troops liberated the area from the Nationalists in 1948, the populace had already become familiar with many of the Party's key stances. Land reform proceeded smoothly, in most villages, as did collectivization in 1956. The Party built a solid reputation for effectiveness in the first decade of its rule, but the Great Leap Forward, beginning in 1958, ended this quickly. Zealous Party cadres, at directions from above, created unmanageable communes (three times the present size) and centralized ownership over land and production equipment. They forced peasants to use new, untried methods of production, such as deep planting, many of which failed. All trees in the entire commune were felled to provide fuel for small blast furnaces which produced unusable pig iron. Food shortages developed, and in 1961 the commune experienced a net drop in population despite the return of many former peasants who returned from cities in search of more food.

The old Party guard disgraced itself in the eyes of many peasants, but the collective system weathered the storm. The commune experienced a moderate recovery of grain output in the early 1960's, but throughout the decade distributable per capita income fluctuated wildly. A low was reached during the Cultural Revolution, when the rate of collective savings was pushed to a new high. By the end of the decade, neither living standards nor productivity had increased much over the standards set in the 1950's.

Only in the 1970's did the commune experience significant changes in income and productivity. Beginning in 1971, the commune began to increase grain yields significantly. Grain yields nearly doubled during the following decade, reaching nearly nine tons per hectare, with the largest increase occuring in 1974 when a new system of "triple cropping" was introduced. (The three plantings and harvests were not consecutive, but were achieved through interplanting in staggered periods.) By the end of the decade, however, it appeared that the potential for further increases in yields had been nearly exhausted.

Income did not rise immediately with the increase in grain yields. In the first half of the 1970's, income stabilized at a level comparable to the 1950's. Only in 1976 did income begin to increase annually, at a rate of about 10%. Nonetheless, the increase in income had nothing to do with increased grain yields. The commune benefitted from its increasing yields of grain in the form of larger grain rations and improved quality of diet (less corn and more wheat and pork). Although the commune's gross income increased with larger grain sales to the state, because of higher production costs associated with the new planting methods, net agricultural income failed to go up. The most expensive production item became chemical fertilizer, which, along with other inputs, erased potential increases in income. Looking at the decade as a whole, grain yields nearly doubled, while gross profit from grain production declined slightly. Profit per unit of output declined sharply.

The increases in distributed income beginning in 1976 are accounted for by the increasing sideline activities in the commune, a characteristic that Dahe commune apparently shares with the village of Kaixiangong described in this volume by Fei Xiaotong. Many brigades and teams set up small enterprises such as brick kilns, sewing shops, casting shops, paper mills, noodle factories, or silk worm raising enterprises. Teams sent their mule carts and 12 horsepower tractors to haul stone from nearby quarries to the city of Shijiazhuang. Many villages set up teams of masons and carpenters to work on temporary contracts at construction sites during the winter slack season in agriculture.

The success of these endeavors has created almost a euphoric feeling about the future, because villagers expect improvements to continue. Already the quality of life in the commune has improved markedly, with collectively owned televisions and movie projectors in all the brigades. But the path to continued advances may not be an easy one. The commune faces a dual set of problems. One involves the choices for further investment, and the other management practices.

Although the political climate was not completely favorable to them, sideline enterprises did develop throughout the 1970's. Now the green light has been given, and sidelines may be developed with full political sanction. But whether villages can continue to discover profitable areas for further investment remains an open question. Brick production has proved to be one of the most profitable enterprises. But by now so many villages have set up large brick kilns that it is difficult to see where they will sell their product. If the state succeeds in its goals of reducing capital construction, this industry could be hard hit. Already in 1979, income from transporting construction materials and from sending out construction teams fell because of a reduced level of building in the area. Many villages have signed contracts for sewing and casting with larger factories in Shijiazhuang, but these activities are relatively unreliable, since factories have been known not to renew contracts.   Helen Siu notes a comparable phenomenon in Huancheng Commune.   Because of this, the teams and brigades do not want to risk a big investment.   Villagers see their best hope for the future in processing their own agricultural produce, such as cotton, silk, and apples.   But if they choose this path, they may end up competing with state-owned enterprises for raw materials, a situation which has recently come under attack in the Chinese press.   Thus, it is by no means clear that the commune will be able to continue its recent dramatic increases in income by continuing to diversify the economy.

With respect to management practices, the commune has made advances in recent years, principally in response to initiatives taken at the national level.   Beginning in the mid-1960's, the production teams adopted a set of management methods associated with the now discredited national model, Dazhai production brigade.   Commune members earned work points from their production teams according to a retrospective evaluation of their efforts for the team, including an assessment of political attitudes.   Although many cadres reported that the system worked reasonably well at first, eventually the system broke down as members were assigned to labor grades, and work point totals and distribution had less and less relationship to work actually performed.   Many peasants slacked on the job.   Managing production teams became much harder for the team heads, since they continually had to prod members to work hard in order to achieve any results at all.

Reforms have now introduced two systems for the teams: the responsibility system and the contract system.   Under the responsibility system, individual team members are assigned a parcel of land and given principal responsibility for tending corn or cotton planted on it.   Their work point totals are then based on the final yield, rather than any calculation of the amount of work performed.   Because of the difficulties of keeping wheat from the harvest separated during threshing and drying, teams generally use a system of awarding points for the tasks accomplished, such as weeding or spraying a specific area.   Team leaders report that work efficiency increased dramatically after these reforms were adopted.   The job of leading a team is also much easier since team members cooperate more readily.

The contract system involves the signing of written contracts between different levels of the system. Individuals sign contracts with their teams, team cadres sign contracts with the brigade, and so on up the line.   The contracts specify bonus pay to be awarded for overfulfilling contracts, penalties for underfulfillment, and the amount of inputs, such as fertilizer and pesticides that the government must supply. Team, brigade and commune cadres too can receive substantial rewards for overfilling the targets for wheat, cotton, and corn production, as well as targets for profit and population growth. The system greatly clarifies the goals toward which cadres are supposed to work, and prevents cadres from placing undo emphasis on some goals for political reasons. For example, it is unlikely that under this system, cadres will have strong incentives to push for increases in grain output over other goals, since the bonus for grain production is not any greater than in other categories. The contract is not legally binding. There is no recourse should the government fail to supply fertilizer on time, but cadres feel that the whole system of management has been greatly rationalized by making everyone's commitment and responsibility more explicit.

These two sets of reforms—the contract and responsibility systems—appear to have greatly improved management. But financial management and economic planning are still very lax. Using the current system of accounting, production teams have no effective way to calculate production costs. In spite of the 1979 increase in the purchase price of agricultural produce, production teams do not earn very much cash income from selling grain to the state. Teams comply with government directives to plant specified crops in specified amounts, and they do not worry very much about the economics of alternate crops or planting methods. Since there is little money to be made in agriculture anyway, and teams have no real choice about what they will plant, many teams don't pay much attention to the possibilities of improving financial management. They try to develop cash-earning sidelines rather than improve the efficiency of agricultural production. This is probably a rational decision from their perspective. But for China as a whole, the cost may be tremendous. The introduction of more rational methods for planning and managing production at the local level is thus an important item for future reforms.

Field Research in China:
Assessing the Potentials

The above description of data gathering and preliminary findings shows at least some of the potentials for what can accomplished by working through the system. As implied and stated repeatedly, I believe that it is impossible to conduct any research by circumventing arrangements that have been made. To what extent do these arrangements affect the quality of fieldwork? Do they require that a field researcher compromise his or her integrity as an individual or as a social scientist, and thereby taint research findings? Unfortunately it is not possible to answer these questions with a categorical "no" because the personal behavior and work style of the researcher will directly affect how cooperative his or her hosts will be in helping to gather data.

The problem, of course, is not by any means unique to China. In any field situation, researchers are critically dependent on cooperation from other people to gather data. People who are suspicious, feel offended, or are very busy generally cooperate less. China is no different in this respect, but the way in which the Chinese government structures and controls access to data may present special problems. In other societies where field research is possible, the foreign researcher usually has some degree of control over selecting the organization or population to be studied. If the research subject proves inaccessible or uncooperative for some reason, it is always possible to redesign a study and select a subject that is more cooperative. But in China, actual research situations, and organizations and populations for study are arranged and selected by units to which the researcher is joined. Before even gaining initial access to research subjects, a researcher must learn to elicit cooperation from the unit to which he or she is attached. If these units conclude that a researcher is "unfriendly," that access may be affected. Whether the structure of access to data presents a constraint or a potential to be exploited depends very much on the researcher.

The first, and most obvious, possible problem that comes to mind is political constraint. Will the Chinese insist that a researcher must be supportive of or sympathetic to China's socialist system, or communist ideology, before helping to open doors? The simple answer to this question is no, but the researcher's attitude toward Chinese socialism and the Chinese revolution does make a difference. The people that most field researchers will be working with are Communist Party members who genuinely believe in socialism. At the same time, all of them are aware that their socialist system has not performed up to expectations. Each may have a differing explanation as to the reason, but many Party members are a little defensive about the value of socialism per se. I was asked on occasion if I felt that China would be better off dividing up land among peasants and allowing private farming to develop. I feel certain that it was a leading question, and that people were testing me to see if, having come from a capitalist country, I had any "understanding" of the value of socialism. I was able to answer honestly that I did not feel that dividing up the land made much sense at this point, but there are sound reasons, based on the experience of other nations, for arguing that collective agriculture cannot out-perform the private family farm. Had I answered that private family farming is a superior system for China, as many agricultural economists undoubtedly would have, I am sure it would have raised the suspicions of my hosts. They would have wondered whether I was not simply looking for factual material to discredit China's commmune system.

Officials from the foreign affairs offices of the province and prefecture often stressed to me that they hoped my visit would promote friendship between the Chinese and American people, and that when I returned to America, I would present an "accurate" picture of life in China's countryside. Both of these goals are laudable, but the continual repetition of these themes revealed that my hosts were indeed worried that I would be overly harsh in my criticisms, and not lavish enough in my praise, that my analysis would be one-sided, criticizing shortcomings but not recognizing achievements and good intentions. I went to some trouble to convince my hosts that I did not have any deep hostility toward Chinese socialism, and that I too wanted my views to be accurate, objective, and constructive, although I made certain that at the same time I did not express any blanket support for socialism or Marxism. I do feel that in the end my hosts accepted the fact that I would form my views independently. They did not expect me to endorse socialism, only to "understand" it, and I think I was able to preserve my integrity. But there will likely be many social scientists, whose views differ from mine, who will not be quite so comfortable in the situation in which I found myself. They will feel pressured to express opinions they do not believe, and may feel that they have been offered a choice between compromising themselves and risking the full cooperation of local officials. This problem is clearly one that each social scientist must wrestle with individually.

Having said this, however, it must be added that every official I met in China expressed what I think is a sincere desire for criticisms of their work. They are looking for suggestions on how to solve some of the obvious and difficult problems they face, and the range of criticisms they accept as "constructive" is fairly broad. They did not mind my pointing out that the status of men and women is vastly unequal, even after they repeatedly told me otherwise. They accepted with enthusiasm my view that agricultural prices in

China are way too low, and thought that it was very helpful when I told them that their bookkeeping and statistical system was a mess because it prevented any meaningful analysis of economic performance and, consequently, prevented them from rationally planning improvements in management.   In other words, they will accept virtually any criticisms and suggestions on how to tinker with their system as long as these criticisms do not question the premises of the system, the social goals of the government, or the good intentions of the people who staff it.

Aside from the political environment in which he works, the researcher must develop a sensitivity to the tremendous burden which he places on the units that he studies, a fact that Burton Pasternak has also noted. The foreign researcher will use a great deal of everyone's time, much of which is indirect and hidden from view, as in the long hours of meetings that will inevitably be held to discuss how to deal with a "foreign guest." He or she may also present a financial burden to the host institution. Some of these burdens can be paid for, and should be, but money cannot buy good will. The researcher needs to recognize the burden he imposes, and make at least a gesture to contribute something in return. This can be done in many ways that are surprisingly easy. I taught English twice a week in the evenings to some of the high school English teachers in the area. I know that this was appreciated enormously since English is now the principal foreign language studied in Chinese schools, yet there is still a great lack of qualified teachers.

But the bulk of "repaying" a host institution and its staff goes beyond simple exchange into learning how to operate within China's cultural system. Mastery of the system entails learning a set of roles and tailoring behavior so that you do not exceed the bounds of what is expected from someone in your role. The role of social science field researchers is that of a "foreign guest." We have such a category in Western society, but it is quite different from the role I was expected to play in a remote Chinese village. The area where the commune was located had not received any foreign visitors since Japanese troops left at the end of the Second World War. In fact, visits by officials from a level of government higher than the county were extremely rare, and the villages may never have been visited by officials from the central government. Thus, my stay in the commune along with the officals who came with me or who came to visit me was extremely unusual. Villagers and their leaders clearly felt that they were participating in an important national event that had ramifications for Sino-American relations and

China's overall position in the world. They felt that I was
a very powerful person of some sort in my own society, and
that my visit to the village was an important part of China's
national policy, directly sanctioned by the central
government. This was a very heavy responsibility which they
could not take lightly, and local officials and people of the
commune went to great lengths to see that I was taken care of
in a manner appropriate to my perceived stature. At first I
thought that the kind of treatment I received was encouraged
by the foreign affairs officials, but later I concluded that
it was simply an outpouring of the best hospitality that
people could offer, as though a populist minded President
descended on a rural backwater to attend a "town meeting."
Even toward the end of my stay, I could not enter the common
room where commune cadres watched television in the evening
without having everyone stand up and not sit down again until
I was seated.

To complain about such treatment makes you look like an
ungrateful guest and makes people feel that they have been
bad hosts. Rather than fight it, it is better to play along.
It works out better for everyone. I became convinced toward
the end of my stay that even ordinary Chinese peasants
perceived of the way I was treated as role playing, in the
fullest sociological sense, and part of an elaborate ritual.
The status conferred on me was not intrinsic to myself, but
derived from the roles played in a situation that was really
beyond anyone's control. When I played along, it put people
more at ease. They felt they knew what they could expect
from me and could relax. Part of playing the exalted guest
involved participating in an elaborate system of ritual
etiquette--with enthusiasm. At banquets, it is important
that the guest be able to raise high toasts to Sino-American
friendship, and propose toasts to each individual that affirm
the special contribution each has made to the project.
Guests must always be happy. They must be cheerful,
friendly, outgoing, and tireless. They must be able to
convey some magic of the role to all those with whom they
come into contact. A guest must take nothing for granted and
continually express thanks for all that is done for him. The
Chinese brush off the thanks with a remark that they are only
doing their job or what is expected of them, but reassurance
that they are pleasing their guest is important. Behavior in
the manner I have just outlined can be extremely tiring, but
there is no real alternative if you want to make the research
experience as positive as possible for the Chinese who help
you.

But in addition to accepting the role into which he is
cast, it is also very valuable for a researcher to be humble

and hard working. I believe this is also quite unexpected by
the Chinese. I wore plain clothing and lived as simply as my
hosts would let me. I did as much work for myself as I
could, such as washing my clothes by hand, and I walked or
rode my bicycle rather than accept a ride. Many people came
up to me and said that they liked this do-it-yourself
attitude, and I came to sense that they would not expect it
from their own high officials. People in the village found
it refreshing and this was communicated back to me in many
ways. Chinese peasants feel that their villages, homes, and
standards of living are extremely humble, and they had real
respect for my effort to adapt as well as I could. They told
me that they had expected me to run back into the city every
weekend for a hot bath and a night in a warm room. I made a
special effort to be continually cheerful when conducting
household surveys, and word came back to me through commune
officials that I had "made a good impression" on people.
That sort of reaction is very helpful for making people feel
that they have not taken on their burden in vain.

But in addition to understanding the behavioral
expectations placed on a foreign guest, it is also very
valuable for a guest to understand the complicated social
system into which he has placed himself, and to learn how to
help and support people within that system. Revolution or
no, Chinese society is highly stratified, and in any
collection of leaders, there will be a fairly clear pecking
order. At banquets, toasts need to be raised first to the
highest ranking person, even if that person is not especially
important as far as the research project is concerned. These
persons must also be invited to the banquet that a researcher
gives and be given top honors. But the presence of unusually
high ranking officials in a basic level administrative unit
also gives the researcher an opportunity to pat local cadres
on the back in front of their superiors. About mid-way
through my research I received a visit from an administrative
cadre from the foreign affairs section of the Academy of
Social Sciences. He was accompanied by an official from the
prefecture. By this time, I had begun to understand a little
about inter-unit dynamics in the Chinese political system. I
had learned enough to know that everyone from Peking to the
village was a little insecure and uncertain about how well my
project was going, or whether they had accommodated me well.
Although I did not especially like visits from outside,
because they tended to slow down my research, I made a point
to welcome this cadre with great decorum. I invited him to
come along on my interviews to see how well things had been
going, and later had long discussions with him about the
progress of my research. The next day we had a banquet for
him, which I used to display the cordial, relaxed relation-

ships which I had developed with all the local cadres. The numerous toasts provided plenty of opportunity to praise everyone for the important contribution they had made to the success of my research. The cadre from the Academy left for Peking feeling that he had been well entertained, that my project was proceeding well, that local cadres had been doing an excellent job helping me out, and, most important, that his own work arranging my field research had been successful. The local cadres, in turn, were pleased because I had made them look very good in the eyes of someone whom they regarded as influential. It is by taking advantage of opportunities like this that the researcher can find ways to reduce the heavy burden which he places on almost everyone with whom he comes into contact.

The point here is that the system does present a number of constraints on the activities of researchers, but that these constraints can be reduced, and the potentials for research maximized if a researcher learns to operate effectively in the social and cultural milieu. This does not mean that a researcher need espouse political principles that he does not believe, but it clearly requires that he learn, accept, and participate in an elaborate, ritualistic society that places him in a role that many will find extremely uncomfortable. It demands that a researcher become personally involved with and committed to the people around him, not simply a detached observer gathering data. It means that research projects that involve gathering data in geographically dispersed units may be difficult to execute because of the time involved in establishing personal relations with cadres, and earning their confidence. A researcher must immerse himself fully into the complex web of social relations that characterize any Chinese organization. In short the researcher must take the time and make the effort to become a full member of the system that he comes to study. The rewards for doing so can be rich. He may return home with a vast amount of valuable data gathered with the help of local cadres who have come to trust him. He has a unique opportunity to gain an insider's view of a society that has been hidden from us for a very long time. And for the fortunate, learning the ritual will provide a new set of tools for communicating with the people around him, breaking down the political and cultural barriers that separate two peoples, making it possible to build deep and satisfying friendships with the people he studies and with whom he has worked so closely.

6. Taitou Revisited: Prospects for Community Restudies

In 1945, Martin Yang (Yang Mo-qun), then working in the Anthropology Department at Columbia University, published a book called A Chinese Village: Taitou, Shantung Province.[1] The book described his native village, the place he had lived until his teens, and which he continued to visit yearly during his college days in Jinan and Peking. After graduation, Yang taught rural sociology at Chilu University in Jinan, Shandong, continuing to maintain contact with his home community. Even after he came to the United States for advanced graduate work, Yang stayed in touch with his native place. His book is based both on some fieldwork as well as on memories, general observations, and information received in letters from relatives and friends. In 1979-80, upon being invited to teach at Shandong University in Jinan, I requested and gained permission to do a restudy of the same community with the intention of bringing its history up-to-date and perhaps revising some of Yang's earlier descriptions.

This paper addresses two problems which are, I think, interrelated. The first is the set of constraints facing researchers who hope to do field level investigations in the People's Republic of China: to what extent will such field researchers have free access to information, written documents, and informal opportunities for observation and participation in daily life? The second problem is the set of constraints on rural development: to what extent does the degree of development or backwardness of a rural community reflect natural local conditions and village leadership ability and to what extent bureaucratic rules and decisions?

---

1. Martin C. Yang, A Chinese Village: Taitou, Shantung Province (New York: Columbia University Press, 1945).

Constraints on Field Research

As both Anne Thurston and Burton Pasternak point out in
·their contributions, not only was social science research in
China curtailed during the years of the Cultural Revolution
(1966-1976), but the techniques, approaches and theories of
contemporary sociology and social anthropology had already
been rejected or laid aside as inappropriate by the decade of
the 1950's. The example set by Mao in his investigation
into the peasant movement in Hunan, the village
investigations by revolutionary cadres during the Yenan
period and the civil war, or the land reform period of the
late 1940's and early 1950's, were praised but not continued.
"Going down to the countryside to learn from the peasants"
came to mean one of two things. Either it meant a period of
labor in the countryside (with punitive connotations during
the Cultural Revolution) or it meant a short visit to a
particular model unit for purposes of describing and hailing
its achievements, contrasting the sweetness of the present
with the bitter past.

Thus, my request for five months in a rural village was
met with considerable puzzlement. Clearly, I was not "going
down" to be reformed by labor but to gather material for
publication. Then why should I need five months in one
village? Why not five months in twenty-five villages? Would
that not be more useful? After all, my contacts explained,
"when you go to the countryside to make on-the-spot
investigations you need no more than three or four days.
Sometimes one day is enough. You talk to the brigade cadres,
you visit one or two typical peasant families, you'take a
look around the village and then you go away."

Such a reaction is understandable given the moratorium
on sociological research over the past twenty years or so.
Only in China's minority areas has there been a continuation
of social research paralleling that in other parts of the
world. Sociology had not been taught in the universities
since 1952. The sociological surveys, community studies, and
social science research work of the pre-revolutionary period
had long ceased to be required readings for anyone in China.

Thus it should come as no surprise that of the leaders
with whom I spoke in the area where Taitou is located, none
were aware of the existence of Yang's study. Nor were the
people of Taitou. More than forty years have passed since
Yang was there. When he returned to China at the end of
World War II, that region of Shandong had already been
liberated and he was unable or unwilling to visit. Today,
Yang is only vaguely remembered. The village history,

compiled in the early 1970's, notes that there was one
college graduate from the village prior to Liberation. No
one seemed to know what happened to him.

The reaction of the higher-level authorities to learning
that there was an earlier book about Taitou was that I had
best not mention it. They were concerned that it would
create problems for that portion of the village population
whose surname is Yang. Yet it is impossible to write about
Taitou's path of development without some reference to the
earlier study, or to pretend to my China colleagues in the
States that the village I studied has no relation to the
village described in the monograph still assigned in most of
our classes.

Remaining silent about the book while in Taitou required
some modification of what I had hoped to do in the field and
posed difficulties in my attempts to clarify and revise some
of Yang's assertions and interpretations. It would have been
interesting, for instance, to follow up on Yang's rich
discussions of lineage-based factionalism and religious
splits in the community, information that is not at all in
evidence in the village history and thus could not be known
to an outsider like me. It would also have been interesting
to work with Yang's rich detailing of family life and living
standards, descriptions which I have always suspected were an
idealized representation of rich peasant/landlord lifestyles,
but there was no way, without alluding to the book, directly
to introduce these data for evaluation and commentary by
former rich peasants, middle peasants and poor peasants.

Indeed, talking about the pre-Liberation past at all
proved to be difficult unless the purpose was to demonstrate
the poverty, exploitation and suffering that existed before
the revolution. The past has been mythologized in a sense.
It can only be discussed in negative terms. No nostalgia for
any features of earlier days seems to exist, or at least such
nostalgia was rarely expressed by informants during my
interviews with them. But those with whom I was encouraged
to discuss the past were former poor peasants, tenants, and
hired laborers for whom the past has little in the way of
pleasant memories.

I eventually was able to interview a fairly wide range
of people, including some of the former rich peasants in the
village. However, all the interviews were arranged for me by
the brigade leadership who always had to be advised in
advance about the topics to be covered in the interview.
Moreover, the interviews were not private. In the first few
weeks of field research, I was accompanied not only by an

interpreter assigned by the Foreign Affairs Office and at
least one member of the brigade leadership but also by a
representative from the District Foreign Affairs Office.
Even after the district representative was persuaded to
return to more pressing work, one or two members of the
brigade leadership always accompanied me. Clearly, it was
useful to have village representatives arrange interview
times and assure that people were released from their work
assignments without being penalized financially. It was also
useful to have a prominent member of the community arrange
introductions. But such close involvement by brigade level
leadership also created a situation which violates the ethics
under which anthropologists normally work. We have been
told, throughout our training, that anthropological ethics
require us to protect the identity and privacy of our
informants. Certainly one does that in writing up field
data. If interviews are in some sense "public," as in this
case, the researcher can protect informants only by not
asking them about certain things, by avoiding potentially
controversial topics. Yet one fears that even with the
exercise of utmost discretion, one cannot fully protect one's
informants. There is that nagging thought that something
asked in innocence and responded to with candor might in the
future be held against them. No clear guidelines about what
is permissible to discuss with foreigners exist. And
political shifts may make yesterday's acceptable remark
tomorrow's heresy.

Yet both the constraints of time and my living
arrangements required local assistance in scheduling
interviews. My fieldwork had to be broken into several
segments of short duration. My primary purpose for being in
China was to teach, and my field time was thus limited to the
two months preceding the start of the school year, the
one-month winter break, and the summer following the school
year. Some of that time was spent in a second village, an
advanced model unit which I had visited for a week in 1977.
Since Taitou is an average village for Shandong Province, the
provincial authorities were rather firm in their suggestion
that I make a revisit to Shijiazhuang brigade near Anqiu.
The experience of seeing how much further along they had come
was rewarding, but it limited field time in Taitou to a
little under four months. By the usual standards of
anthropological fieldwork, four months is a very short time
indeed, not really sufficient for forming friendships,
establishing rapport, and becoming an accepted member of the
community.

However, living arrangements were not under my control,
and double the field time would not have enabled me to blend

more easily into the community. On the first summer visit, I was placed in the district guesthouse located ten kilometers from Taitou, an arrangement which required a car and a driver and necessitated returning to the guesthouse for lunch. Moreover, this arrangement limited my work to the daylight hours. On the two subsequent visits, I was allowed to stay in a room in the commune center, a fifteen minute walk from Taitou, but evening visits were discouraged. There seemed to be no way to gain permission to live in the village, eat in the village, be there on a round-the-clock basis, and to interact informally and casually with the villagers.

To some extent, the living arrangements and the lack of casual access to the village had to do with how my presence in China was defined. My impression is that scholars who were then in China under the official exchange program run by the Committee on Scholarly Communication with the People's Republic of China had less difficulty in obtaining permission to live in the community or unit they were researching. I had expected that Shandong University would sponsor my field work and that I would be allowed to take a number of students with me to the field at some point to conduct a wide range of interviews. However, for the first summer of research, the university refused to act as sponsor, ostensibly because I had not yet begun teaching for them. Thus, all arrangements, including the choice of a field assistant, were left to the Provincial Foreign Affairs Office, the Qingdao Foreign Affairs Office, and, at the lowest level, the Huangdao District Foreign Affairs Office. At winter break, I was allowed to take two students with me, and in the final segment, a young teacher from the Languages Department.

I detail these problems primarily because researchers who go to China on grants from private foundations or who hope to combine research with a work assignment there may well experience similar difficulties. Such scholars should be forewarned that field research in China is unlikely to be the same protracted and independent endeavor portrayed in the classic ethnographies. China is not overly enthusiastic about having foreign social scientists poking around, and those who come without official U.S. government sponsorship (and without a special ombudsman in the embassy to intervene if they run into difficulties in their work) should not expect doors to open easily. Of course, as social science continues to develop in China, it is possible that the attitude toward foreign researchers will change and there will be more interest in cooperative projects, training students in field techniques, and in the inputs that such research might make toward China's development.

Given the difficulties I have just described, I am
nonetheless pleased with the amount of data that I was able
to collect, and with the level of cooperation from the
brigade level cadres and members of the village community.
After discussion as to my purpose, I was allowed to copy the
household records for the entire village, thus obtaining
materials on household size and composition, marriage age,
and some material on educational levels. I was allowed to
look at and copy the workpoint records for the work teams,
the economic records of the work teams, and brigade summary
sheets on production, costs, and distribution for the 1960's
and 1970's.

Some written records, particularly those materials
pertaining to land reform, the early mutual aid teams and the
early cooperatives, had been destroyed by visiting Red Guards
during the Cultural Revolution. But the Red Guards had not
been able to destroy them all, and using those records that
had been preserved, together with the pooled memories of
older members of the village, it was possible to reconstruct
the process of initial land division, the class composition
of the village on the eve of the revolution, the composition
and basis for the mutual aid teams, and the composition of
the first cooperatives. Indeed, it was both rewarding and
enjoyable to sit together with five or six older people who
had participated actively in these events and together
reconstruct that period of village history.

It was also fairly easy to run a series of household
interviews on family income from both collective and private
sources and family budgeting for daily life and special
occasions (weddings, house building, etc.), selecting a range
of households on the basis of what I already knew about them
from the household records and team accounts. Of the
households I selected for the sample, only two or three
proved impossible to interview because, as the leadership
told me, it was "inconvenient". And it was possible, going
through the village school, to interview the parents of most
of the children in one of the higher grades. Visiting at New
Year's time provided a good opportunity to talk about kinship
networks, the obligations that kin relations entail, and
social relationships with non-kinsmen. Some households were
revisited more often than others to talk about such matters
as informal cooperation between households, the problems of
arranging marriages for one's children, and the like. As the
work continued, the brigade leaders became more receptive to
the idea that social research involves more than just the
bare economic facts about production and average incomes.

Taitou Village Revisited

The Village of Taitou and Its
Relations with Its Environs

Let me turn now from this discussion of what fieldwork
in China is like to a consideration of the village itself.
For those unfamiliar with Yang's earlier study, Taitou is
located in the recently created Huangdao district in
southeastern Shandong, across the bay from the city of
Qingdao. Yang had assumed that Taitou would become more
tightly linked to the city in the postwar period, but in
actuality the linkage was broken when Taitou and its environs
were liberated in late summer of 1945. Qingdao continued to
be held by the Guomindang, with the aid of American naval
forces, until June of 1949. Jiao County, where Taitou was
located, became linked to the rest of the liberated area and
was made part of Changwei region, with the city of Weifang,
far to the north, as its key municipality. It was not a
total break with Qingdao. During the 1950's, people from
Taitou still continued some private marketing in the city;
some young people attended secondary school and technical
schools in Qingdao; and a small number of villagers
continued, as they had earlier, to work in Qingdao factories
and enterprises. However, after 1958, and particularly after
the start of the Cultural Revolution in 1966, the cleavage
became wider. Youth who had received advanced education in
Qingdao were returned to the village. The system of rural
household registration (hukou) was strengthened, preventing
migration from rural to urban areas either by individuals or
by the family members of those who had received an urban
hukou. And at no time in the post-Liberation period was
Taitou's region included in the economic planning for the
city. Qingdao suburbs were defined as the areas lying to its
east and north.

Contrary to Yang's predictions, then, Taitou did not
become a suburb of Qingdao. On a clear day, standing at an
elevated point near the village, one can see the city across
the bay, but Qingdao might as well have been in another
province. Taitou's city was Weifang, a journey of 60
kilometers over mountain roads to the nearest railroad link
at Jiao County and another four or five hours by train. Not
until 1977 was the Huangdao District, a portion of the former
Jiao County, reassigned to Qingdao and incorporated into the
municipality. Technically speaking, Taitou is now a suburban
commune. But it still bears the marks of a village in the
far hinterland of Weifang — a grain producing village with
very little cash cropping, a low level of mechanization,
little diversification of agricultural sideline production,

and almost no industrial sideline enterprises of its own. Compared to Shijiazhuang brigade, which is an hour's drive from Weifang over paved roads and fifteen minutes from the growing industrial town of Anqiu, or, apparently, with Huancheng Commune described in this volume by Helen Siu, Taitou is a poor village. For Shandong as a whole it is average. By overall national standards it is better than average. In light of what Yang says about the village in earlier times it bears the marks of underdevelopment. Taitou, in some ways, has regressed.

The market-town at Xingan, now the commune center for Taitou and its neighbors, is no longer the bustling place that Yang describes. The four inns are gone, only one of several of the restaurants survives, and the drugshops, silversmiths and bakeries have all vanished. So have the two wineries. Only a handful of shops remain to service the 39,000 commune members. The periodic five day market resumed in 1977 as an outlet for peasant produce and handicrafts, but has nowhere near the variety of goods described by Yang. Nearby Wantai, a large market town that in earlier times boasted numerous small industries, seems also to have declined and has ceased to be the market or source for luxury goods and special items that Yang described.[2]

Though Taitou is now technically reunited with Qingdao, the metropolis is hard to reach. Until 1980, ferry service across the bay was minimal: one ferry per day, leaving in mid-morning and returning in early afternoon, giving little time to conduct one's business in town. And the cost was prohibitive--the equivalent of three day's earnings for a peasant.

The better prospect for the suburbanization of Taitou lies with the new industrial center planned for the town of Huangdao, which is the site of the new oil port for the Shengli oilfields. The current projected size for the town is 45,000. It will be linked by rail to Jiao County, and one spin-off of the development of the new center will be an increase in ferry service to Qingdao. Some Qingdao factories will be relocated in Huangdao or will establish branches there. Town jobs, I was told, will be limited to people with urban household registrations. During the time I was there some 3,000 workers were brought in from Jinan. Only two of the brigades in the district had received assignments to grow vegetables to supply to Huangdao. Most of the produce was still being trucked in from Jiao County. Presumably this

---

2. *Ibid.*, pp. 190-191.

policy will change, and Huangdao's rural units will eventually be supplying vegetables, fruits, eggs, meat, and fish to the urban center, but at present writing they are doing so only through the private market.

The Local Economy

For Huangdao as a whole, in 1979-80, the emphasis was on growing grain, with 74% of cropland devoted to grain production. Because of the quality of the soil and problems with water, sweet potatoes still make up close to half of the summer crop. Altogether, about 18% of the land in summer was used for the cash cropping of peanuts. In the summer of 1979, the estimated average incomes for the district's agricultural villages ranged from 85 yuan per capita per year in the poorest to around 140 yuan per annum in the wealthiest. Taitou's average income then was 134 yuan per capita. Incomes ran higher in the maritime brigades involved with fishing, kelp production, and tank-raising of abalone and beche-de-mer—as high as 300 yuan per person.

Xingan Commune, of which Taitou is a part, had little industrial development in 1979-80. Commune level industries employed only 600 persons, or about 1.5% of the population. Expansion was planned for the commune-operated shrimp farm. Some specialized industries or sidelines had begun to operate at brigade levels since reunification with Qingdao: about ten brigades had contract arrangments for women to do piecework embroidery in their homes for sale to city factories. Xingan's richest brigade grew vegetables for sale to Huangdao and four others were allowed to sell vegetables to state purchasing units. One brigade had fish ponds, whose produce was sold through a state purchasing and retailing unit in the commune center. Another five brigades had begun raising oysters in salt water ponds.

Taitou in 1979-80 was an average unit within Xingan Commune. It consisted of 204 households, a population of around 970, and a cultivated area of 1,302 mu. Physically, it still bears some resemblance to Yang's description, but there have been some major changes. The Pearl River, formerly a source of periodic flooding, has been rechanneled and its bed widened. The new area between the river and the beginning of the settlement has been converted into fruit orchards and land for private plots. A large cistern has been built for irrigation purposes; new wells have been dug; and a few pump wells have been introduced. Virtually all the housing is now of stone, brick and tile construction, and the newer housing is laid out in neat parallel streets. Most houses now have privies separate from the pig-sty. These are all post-Liberation developments.

Even at the time of Liberation, the land per capita ratio was low. The population then was 650 persons, and the goal of land reform, roughly achieved, evened out holdings to two mu per person. That leveling, in contradiction to national level policies, required confiscation of land not only from the one remaining landlord household but also from Taitou's six rich peasant households and a few households classified as middle peasants. But having a bit more land did not solve the economic problems of many families, and the response to the call for small mutual aid teams was enthusiastic. Virtually every household participated, including the former rich peasant households. Enterprises that had belonged to former landlords and rich peasant families, such as oil press shops, a blacksmithy, a grain mill, and the beancurd factory were run as cooperative ventures. Some individuals continued to work as masons, carpenters, and furniture makers or small traders.

The call for formation of agricultural cooperatives did not receive the same enthusiastic response. Only 18 out of a possible 160 households participated in the lower-level Agricultural Producers' Cooperative. But in 1956-57, when the higher-level Agricultural Producers' Cooperative was organized, membership was mandatory.

Throughout the decade of the 1950's, agricultural production was varied and replicated pre-Liberation patterns. There was some wheat production, but the main staples were millet, kaoliang, corn, and sweet potatoes. Some land was devoted to vegetable production, and peanuts and soybeans were grown as cash crops.

According to Yang's observations for the pre-Liberation period, wheat was grown only by those wealthier households who had access to the best land and a supply of fertilizer, and even they grew secondary crops of millet and kaoliang. The majority of families whose holdings were on lower quality land and small in size concentrated on sweet potatoes as their staple crop. This, together with peanuts and soybeans as cash crops accounted for 60% of the land use. Another 30% was devoted to millet and kaoliang, and a small amount to barley and corn and miscellaneous grains. Since double-cropping was possible, there was summer land for a wide variety of vegetables. Yang mentions cabbages, turnips, onions, garlic, leeks, radishes, cucumber, spinach, several varities of green beans, squashes, peas, coriander, and melons.

I note this in detail because, as Taitou moved into the decade of the 1960's, vegetable production was phased out except for what was grown on private plots. Millet and kaoliang were also discouraged except in small amounts for household distribution. Directives for the area emphasized the importance of wheat and corn. By 1970 the growing of corn was mandatory, at the expense of peanut and soybean production or other crops that had high market value (such as melons, cotton, and vegetables). I do not pretend to be an expert on agricultural planning, but there is some question in my mind as to the suitability of this micro-region for wheat production. Huangdao has an odd maritime climate. Compared to other parts of Shandong, it is cooler in summer, warmer in winter, and rather damp. Fogging is heavy in the mornings, and the fog sometimes does not lift until 10:00 a.m. Though wheat is usually a higher-yield crop than millet and kaoliang, such is not necessarily the case in Taitou.

In the first years of the commune, 48% of the winter crop area was assigned to wheat, a figure which increased to 80% of the crop area after the start of the Cultural Revolution. Millet production had yielded up to 350 jin per mu. With field construction, improved seeds, increase in fertilizer, water inputs, and lesser attention to other crops, wheat production rose. By 1970, it was up to 235 jin per mu, and production hit a high of 346 in 1974. In 1979, team records indicate a variance between 278 to 323 jin per mu. In comparison, wheat yields in the Anqiu area, which has a better suited climate and better water control and double-cropping of wheat, have a variance of from 800 to 1200 jin per mu.

The corn crop does somewhat better, between 450 and 550 jin per mu. Anqiu yields are closer to 800. In the early days of the commune, a third of brigade summer land was assigned to corn. Later, this increased to one-half. The seed strains provided are not regarded locally as desirable for human consumption, although the problem may simply be a lack of knowledge about proper processing. However, the corn is highly valued as animal fodder and its presence has increased household levels of pig production.

Sweet potatoes continue to be a major household staple, though their consumption has been reduced or has disappeared entirely in other areas of Shandong. In Taitou's richest team, the 1978 grain distribution per person consisted of 132 jin of wheat, 174 jin of sweet potatoes, 200 jin of corn, plus 10 jin of soybeans, and 12 jin of peanuts. Each person also received a small amount of millet—less than five pounds. Within the total brigade, wheat made up 25% of the grain available for distribution. It is appreciated as a more prestigious food which was not often eaten except by wealthier families in pre-Liberation days. Still, the villagers I interviewed expressed a desire for greater quantites of millet and kaoliang, which are used in the preparation of the special foods served at New Years Festival and other holidays. Millet is also regarded as a special food for pregnant women, for small children, and for the ill and elderly. Some households meet the need by using a portion of their private plots to grow additional grains. On the private market, these grains were selling at a price higher than that of wheat because of demand and shortage.

These changes in local cropping patterns were not voluntarily decided by Taitou or other local units. They do provide income through the sale of wheat and corn to the state and they have helped to increase pig and poultry production within the community. These are the positive aspects of the planning. On the negative side, the local diet now has less variety in grain, is lower in vegetables and oil than in earlier times, and the pressures to raise corn and wheat production to the levels reached in other areas have absorbed the full attention of the labor force at the expense of diversification. With only 5% of the land in soybeans, the beancurd factory has become defunct. The cotton crop of the 1950's and early 1960's no longer exists. Peanut production has declined sharply even though brigade and team accounts show no reduction of land area. At the start of the Cultural Revolution, Taitou was raising over 95,000 jin of peanuts and selling close to 56,000 to the state. By 1974, production had declined to 63,000 jin of which 29,000 were sold to the state. By 1979, this was further reduced to a total production of 39,000 jin, of which 7,000 could be sold to the state. There are two possible explanations for this dramatic decline. One is that interplanting of sweet potatoes on peanut land has been intensified in order to meet grain needs. The other possibility, which has surfaced in the Chinese press in 1980-81 in criticisms of some rural units, is that the assigned land may actually have been used for grain production as a way of satisfying higher-level authorities that grain-per-mu productivity was on the upswing.

Whatever the reasons, Taitou's potential income is reduced. Sweet potatoes have no market value to speak of. Corn, until the price increases put into effect in 1980, sold for around .08 yuan per jin and wheat for .12 yuan. Peanuts, on the other hand, sold for .21 yuan per jin. Taitou accounts indicate that they sell around 33% of their wheat and corn to the state, but these low income crops do not provide much surplus for investment and diversification of the collective economy.

Utilization of the Labor Force

Brigade records show a total of 430 persons in the active work force of whom 196 are women. This, however, refers more to potential than to actual performance by women in the collective sector. Relatively little seems to have changed since the time described in Yang's volume. The processing of the sweet potato crop, which is done entirely by women, is a household rather than a collective activity, and is unpaid. Women are most involved in the collective sector at harvest and threshing times, but the drying of the grain is conducted on an unpaid household basis. When the peanut crop was more abundant, women did the picking, gleaning, and oil pressing, but with the decline of peanut production, this work has been reduced.

On the basis of the workpoint records kept by the teams, it appears that able-bodied males (who put in some overtime) have an average credit of 350 work days a year. For able-bodied women, the average among those who actually participate is 102 work days credit. If able-bodied women who do not participate are included, the average is 100 work days. The real number of days is somewhat higher, of course: most women cannot earn more than 7 of the possible 10 work points per day because of the press of domestic responsibilities. Women must still take time out to draw water, to do the laundry, prepare meals, tend to the household's livestock, and look after the needs of the children and elderly members of the household. The private plot also requires tending and the periodic market must be attended from time to time for buying or selling, though males also participate in both of these activities.

However, women's private labor is crucial to the household budget. The more pigs raised, the higher the household income. In most households, manure sold to the brigade is worth a credit of between 150 and 250 full work days—as much or more than would be gained by having the woman working in the team. The sale of pigs may account for as much as half of a household's real income each year. And given the limited land available and the current pattern of cropping, women's labor in agriculture would be redundant. It might speed up the work but it is doubtful that it would increase grain production by more than a small increment. Its negative effect would be to reduce the value of the workpoint, to decrease household real income, and to decrease the fertilizer supply.

Until other changes are made, women's productive work and service work will continue to be focused on the household rather than incorporated into the collective economy. And the importance of the household economy, in the absence of other options, seems to have had an effect on family composition and living arrangements. There have been reports of the continuation and preference for stem or joint family residence in some rural units. This supposedly frees more women to participate in the collective work force. Elderly members of the household take on many of the domestic tasks, or sisters-in-law can rotate responsibilities so that younger women of the household can earn work points in the team or in brigade industries. I think this is the case in some places, and I will return to this point. But in Taitou there is a preference for nuclear units, reflected in and reinforced by the brigade's housing plans.

Taitou's program for new housing, in operation for over a decade, provides substantially built three room units on the model of what would have been upper-middle peasant housing in the past. There is no change in the basic design. The change is that the houses are constructed side by side in parallel rows on standard plots. There is no way to add rooms as the family grows. Just as housing space is limited, so is courtyard space, which is meant to hold a storage building, a privy, a small vegetable garden, poultry coops, a rabbit hutch, some sitting room for meals in warmer weather, and, of course, the pig sties. Only through family division can the number of pigs be increased, by gaining a new house and additional courtyard space.

Informal cooperation between closely related households continues, of course, even after households have been formally divided. During the harvest season, and during other busy times, such households expect assistance with child care and with the preparation of meals. But during much of the year, the women in each household look to their own domestic chores, which include the care of the household pigs, poultry, private plots, and a host of daily tasks.

Taitou's Political Economy in
Historical Perspective

In some ways, Taitou is a success. Total brigade income has been going up; the average value of distribution has doubled since the early 1970's; the percentage costs of production have risen only slightly over the past decade; and by national standards the brigade is fairly well off. According to recently released figures for 1979, the average national value of distribution per person was 83.4 *yuan*, with a quarter of all units receiving an average below 50, yuan and only 7.6% receiving over 150 yuan.[3] With a reported average of 176 yuan for year-end 1979, Taitou is up there at the top level, although below Shijiazhuang at 250 yuan.

But given Taitou's location and the assets that it had at the time of liberation, it is possible that the village might have fared even better with somewhat different planning. Nationwide, 18% of rural income comes from industrial crops. In Taitou, this figure is only 5%. Nationwide, 57% of income comes from grain crops, reflecting low development of sidelines, while in Taitou the figure is 48%. This figure looks good on the face of it, but Taitou's claim of 38% of income from sidelines is misleading in that it represents income from contract labor in Huangdao and payment for labor on resources owned by other units—it does not reflect internal development of industries and enterprises as is the case for Shijiazhuang.

As mentioned earlier, Taitou was classed as a grain-producing brigade throughout the decades of the 1960's and 1970's. The slogan "take grain as the key link," which was still voiced in 1979, was interpreted at commune, district and county levels (perhaps even higher) in the most literal possible sense, namely that the major or even sole task of a rural unit was to produce more and more grain for state purchase. On the other hand, calls for diversification and "self reliance," which also were made during that period, received narrow interpretation. During that time, Taitou established only a small scale peach and apple orchard. All other village sidelines were retentions from earlier times. The oil-pressing shop was a cooperative reorganization of the three oil shops that existed in Yang's time when peanut oil production was carried out on a larger scale. There was and continues to be a small tool and machine repair shop which is an outgrowth of the blacksmithy. There is a small grain mill for village use. Until the start of the Cultural Revolution there was a carpentry shop, dissolved after a higher level decision that the labor was needed more in grain production than in the manufacture of wheelbarrows, furniture, and farm tools. The small-scale brick-and-tile kiln that had existed previously was suspended after the establishment of the commune by orders from above.

---

3.   "Let Some Localities and Peasants Prosper First," Beijing Review, Jan. 19, 1981, p. 22. The average may be as high as 102 yuan according to information from Professor Robert Dernberger, Department of Economics, University of Michigan.

For the past few years, Taitou's main sideline industry
has been a contract arrangement with a nearby brigade that
owns a stone quarry. Each of Taitou's teams owns two or three
small wooden boats which carry sand and stone from the quarry
to building sites at Huangdao or Qingdao. Taitou's small
tractors and animal-drawn carts are also pressed into service
for this kind of transport work -- this earns between 11,000
yuan and 15,000 yuan for each of the five teams, and
another 10,000 yuan for the brigade. An average of 8
people from each team work each year as short-term contract
workers, either in Huangdao or in one of the factories in
Xingan Commune. Except for a few contract workers, and the
small group working in the orchard, participation in sideline
activities is limited to males. In 1980, a new sideline was
introduced which has provided jobs for another eight or so
young men and women. It is a small printing press operation,
which has involved hiring two "retired" printers from outside
the village to serve as teachers and supervisors of the
enterprise.

Calls for all-round development, diversification of
brigade economic activities, and attention not only to grain
but also to forestry, animal husbandry, agricultural
sidelines, industrial sidelines, and fisheries have certainly
been in evidence in the national press since the end of 1977.
Elsewhere in Shandong, during 1976 and 1977, brigades that
had diversified after meeting some basic level of surplus
grain production were hailed as Dazhai-type advanced units.
Until 1980, when Dazhai as a model fell completely from
grace, the briefing rooms of such brigades, communes, and
counties that had begun to mechanize agriculture and
diversify their economies were decorated with embroidered
banners hailing them as Dazhai-type models. Changwei and
Yantai prefectures both continue to be praised provincially
and nationally for following such a path of development,
although the term "Dazhai" is no longer applied. But in this
corner of Shandong, development has moved more cautiously and
conservatively than in Changwei and Yantai.

Perhaps that is not a totally fair statement for all of
the Huangdao district. The maritime brigades, some of which
are now working under the direction of the Oceanographic
Institute in Qingdao, have been encouraged to engage in such
profitable ventures as kelp farming, mink raising (using
surplus fish as fodder), and tank raising of the high-priced
delicacies mentioned earlier. There are also plans for fish
canneries and processing of dried fish. But this will affect
at most only 28 of the 117 villages in the district, and at
present only a few are involved in these highly profitable
enterprises. As for the agricultural brigades, the response

to the call for mechanization and diversification has lagged behind other regions.

A Comparison of Taitou with Shijiazhuang, A Model Brigade

At this point, for the purpose of comparison, let me refer briefly to Shijiazhuang, the advanced unit I visited. Shijiazhuang brigade has 200 more people than Taitou and about 200 fewer <u>mu</u> of land. Despite these apparent disadvantages, it is a wealthier place. Throughout the 1960's and 1970's, it was permitted to grow tobacco, a highly valuable cash crop, in addition to being urged to grow wheat and corn. Village-level projects for farmland construction, county-level projects for water control and irrigation, and general planning geared to local conditions combined to assure high crop yields and the possibilities for diversification. Over those two decades, Shijiazhuang developed several highly profitable small sideline industries and was able to begin mechanizing agricultural production. By 1980, only a third of the work force was needed in agriculture. Another third was engaged in building and construction, manufacturing their own brick and tiles for that purpose. The remaining third, predominantly drawn from the female sector of the labor force, were employed in the modern poultry farm, the grain mill, the plastics factory and the canvas bag factory owned by the brigade.

The brigade's new housing is a radical departure from past styles. Shijiazhuang's houses are also on small fixed plots in parallel rows, but the houses are two stories high, consisting of six rooms rather than three, and meant for complex families. A family can raise only two or three pigs in the small courtyard, but no one seems to see this as deprivation or a blow to the household economy. In fact, there are no private plots in Shijiazhuang. A wide variety of vegetables are raised collectively and distributed as they come into season. Most of the brigade's pigs, chickens, and rabbits are also collectively raised.

Women are very much involved in the collective economy — in the agricultural teams, in the agricultural sidelines, and increasingly in the developing industrial sidelines. Most of them now receive a full 10 points for a workday, which meant 1.31 <u>yuan</u> a day in 1979 compared to the .50 <u>yuan</u> gained by a Taitou woman accorded 7 work points. A full-time nursery school and kindergarten, which enrolled 75 children in 1979-80, lightens the domestic load, which is further eased by elderly members of the household or exchanges between sisters-in-law. In 1979, Shijiazhuang had a total brigade income of over 900,000 yuan. Taitou's income was 357,923 yuan. Of course, Shijiazhuang is not typical. It is a provincial model, while Taitou is average.

Conclusion

Arriving in Taitou as I did after a two week revisit to Shijiazhuang, I could not help but make comparisons between the two. The District leadership with whom I discussed the disparities tended to attribute them to differences in leadership at the brigade and team levels, to basic natural conditions, and to economic advantages that had existed prior to Liberation. These explanations now seem to me to be as invalid as the tendency of many anthropologists to explain economic development from the perspective of the study of the small community. Anqiu County as a whole is more industrialized, its agriculture more mechanized, its commune and brigade economies more diversified than what is evident in Huangdao. A focus on the small community is insufficient for understanding recent developments in rural China. Decisions regarding the choice of crops, how the land is allocated, where the crops are to be sold, as well as questions of access to water, fertilizer, new seeds, and new technology are beyond the decision making powers of brigade level cadres. Until 1980 these decisions were coming from the commune which in turn was responding to directives from the district or county level or higher. A focus on local community organization and traditional values is insufficient for understanding progress or stagnation in agriculture.

Similarly, the absence or presence of local small industries is related to the constraints on levels of capital accumulation and to the way in which higher levels of leadership interpreted the teaching of the Cultural Revolution regarding production-for-profit and the dangers of returning to the "capitalist road." In Anqiu county, the latter part of the 1960's and the 1970's were years of economic buildup, despite the political climate of the times. But in Taitou's area, those years were ones in which cash cropping was reduced and the number of sidelines diminished. Even after the fall of the "gang of four," when Taitou was reincorporated into Qingdao, it was directed to "take grain as the key link" and to concentrate on grain production. In terms of mechanization and diversification, it is not even on a par with what are considered "backward" units in Anqiu at the present time. It will take Taitou some time to catch up, and by then the brigades in Anqiu county will have moved even further ahead. No doubt local or brigade leadership and local conditions have something to do with disparities between brigades and communes within a given administrative area. But they are not the source of sharp differences between given administrative areas. What is needed to explain local rural development in China is a study of the interpretation and enforcement of policy at the commune, district, county, and prefectural levels within a context of provincial politics and national policies for the rural areas over the past thirty years.

Still, as mentioned earlier, Taitou is above the national average in terms of its per capita collective earnings. It is measureably better off now than before Liberation in terms of general health, education, housing, clothing, food supply for the mass of the population, and access to a number of prestige consumer items such as watches or bicycles. Why diminish its accomplishments by comparing it to an advanced model unit?

I do so in order to make some further points about understanding the meaning of income distribution from the collective, and about the need to look beyond the village unit for spurs to economic development. The wealth of a unit cannot be measured simply by how much is distributed per capita by the collective. Put simply, people in Taitou work more days each year, for a longer number of hours, doing heavier physical labor in order to gain an income that falls 30% below that of Shijiazhuang. Taitou's medical needs are served by two barefoot doctors. Shijiazhuang is the site of a small hospital with five or six regular doctors, a unit shared with neighboring communities. Shijiazhuang's school goes through senior middle level, while Taitou's only provides education through junior middle school. In quality of life as well as in distributed income, there are many disparities, too numerous to mention.

Secondly, Shijiazhuang feels that it is supported in its endeavors by the county and the prefecture under whose jurisdiction it falls. This may be related to the fact that one of the brigade leaders became a member of the County Revolutionary Committee in 1970, and became a vice-secretary of the County Party Committee after the fall of the "gang of four." It is difficult to judge here what is cause and what is effect. But equally, or more importantly, units in Weifang and Anqiu have for many years, even before the fall of the "gang," encouraged rural units to develop small industrial sidelines or agricultural sidelines. State purchasing units such as the Foreign Trade Bureau have played a very active role in assisting local development.

In contrast, there is no one from all of Huangdao on Qingdao's Revolutionary Committee, according to information from district leaders as late as the summer of 1980.[4] Qingdao had had a long standing involvement with Laoshan County, to its east, for foodstuffs and local products. Its production units and purchasing agencies have been slow to reach out to the newly acquired suburbs of Huangdao. And even if they were to reach out to Huangdao, they would be dealing with units that have relatively little left over, after paying production costs and distributing income, for purchasing machinery for new sidelines.

By summer of 1980, Taitou's commune and district level leadership was beginning to talk about allowing brigades to have more of a voice in decisions about land use and crops, about encouraging small scale sidelines that utilize local materials (basketry, pottery, carpentry, etc.) and, if purchasing could be arranged, some diversion of land into cash crops. By 1981, the various household and individual responsibility systems were being encouraged, particularly for brigades that had little other than grain production as the basis of their collective economy. For Taitou, the motivations to adopt the household responsibility system may have been very strong but at present writing no additional data is available. What will happen depends still on decisions made in Qingdao and at the provincial level. If Taitou's leadership, to date, appears less able and less imaginative than that of a place like Shijiazhuang, it is in large part because Taitou's leadership was held back and discouraged from innovative actions for more than twenty years. Local leadership can be only as good as the next highest levels allow it to be, and perhaps policies are now flexible enough to enable villages to develop at a faster rate than in the past three decades.

---

4. Elections for people's governments and congresses had begun in late 1979 but Shandong has lagged behind in this matter. Press reports for December 1980 pointed out that only 33 of over 133 counties, prefectures and municipalities in Shandong had replaced revolutionary committees with elected peoples governments.

7. Ethnographic Fieldwork in Rural Guangdong: The Virtues of Flexibility

For decades, Western social scientists studying the People's Republic of China have based their research on two primary sources: scanty reports and policy statements trickling out of the country—largely in documentary form, but also in the form of reports by visitors—and interviews conducted in Hong Kong with refugees from the mainland. Recently, the prospects for employing a third source, actual fieldwork within China, have improved, and a select few have been allowed to carry on field research for extended periods of time in both rural and urban communities. As a local resident of Hong Kong, my chance to conduct field research in China came early. I have been making field visits to rural Guangdong since 1974.

Thus far, most Western fieldworkers able to avail themselves of new opportunities have preferred long-term visits to particular local units—brigades, hospitals, factories, urban neighborhoods or the like. What I would like to present here, however, is an argument in favor of a somewhat different mode of field research—a series of short visits to different points in a larger social system, such as a commune, spread over a fairly long period of time.

As Martin Whyte suggests in his contribution to this volume, all the methods traditionally employed by scholars doing research on China have limitations and drawbacks. Relying on documentary sources alone, certain topics are simply impossible to investigate. Researchers conducting systematic interviews with refugees have been able to overcome many of the limitations of documentary sources. The work of Parish and Whyte provides an example of the[1] sophisticated methodology developed with such interviews.

---

1. See William L. Parish and Martin King Whyte, <u>Village and Family in Contemporary China</u> (Chicago: The University of Chicago Press, 1978).

143

But this type of research still has drawbacks. Chinese rural communities vary substantially. For example, what may be true of rural communities on the outskirts of cities may not hold true for communities on the periphery of a regional system. Because neither the number of refugees available to be interviewed in Hong Kong nor the type of rural communities they represent are large enough to allow control on such differentiation, generalizations based on refugee reports are often difficult to draw.

In conducting my own research, which I will describe in the second half of this paper, I employed procedures that were based on two assumptions. The first assumption was that socio-economic development in rural China could be understood within a framework which differentiates rural communities on the basis of the regional systems hierarchy described by G. William Skinner.[2] Secondly, policy in China undergoes cyclical changes, and there is an empirically observable relationship between policy cycles and the nature of socio-economic development within rural communities.[3] Had I relied on interviews with refugees in Hong Kong, it would have been very difficult to describe and analyze rural differentiation and its relationship to cyclical change. For such questions, fieldwork is the obvious method of preference.

As other contributions to this volume demonstrate, long-term research in specific local units can be highly rewarding. Nonetheless, this mode of research also presents both practical and theoretical problems. Practically, time is lost simply in adapting to the local cultural and political milieus. If, in addition, bureaucratic restrictions require changes in research goals or methods, the fieldworker is likely to find himself without needed library and other resources. Knowing that his Chinese hosts are unlikely to extend his time in the field to compensate for the delays engendered by these changes, the researcher may become impatient and even aggressive, thereby reinforcing the fears of already sensitive Chinese sponsors.

From a theoretical perspective, even if the researcher

2. See G. William Skinner, editor, The City in Late Imperial China (Stanford, California: Stanford University Press, 1977).
3. See G. William Skinner and Edwin A. Winckler, "Compliance Succession in Rural Communist China: A Cyclical Theory," in Amitai Etzioni, editor, A Sociological Reader on Complex Organizations (New York: Holt, Rinehart and Winston, 1969), pp. 410-439.

is allowed to gather statistical data covering an extended period of time, the data he gathers and the observations he makes will naturally be affected by and will reflect the specific policy phase within which the fieldwork takes place.

My own fieldwork in rural Guangdong provides an alternative to the more typical pattern of a single, extended stay in one research site. From Hong Kong I made multiple visits, over an extended period of time, to a number of rural communities in one Chinese commune. Each visit was used for a different purpose, and each visit built upon what was previously learned. For instance, a series of "social" visits provided an easy context for gathering ethnographic and historical information. More formal research visits allowed me to collect important statistical data. Repeated trips made over a period of several years enabled me to observe and measure changes associated with shifts in policy and personnel. Moreover, knowing that I would return again to the field, I felt less compelled to squeeze out as much information as possible from any single field trip.

While it is probably easier for an overseas Chinese researcher to make use of this method, I have the impression that comparable opportunities, to some extent, are now opening to others. Several Western field researchers have found it both possible and useful to make follow-up visits after completion of initial long-term field research. The following description of my own experience should illustrate both the strengths and weaknesses of this form of research.

Research Purpose

My research in China has focused on the development of commune and brigade level enterprises. Although rural industrialization—the creation of an industrial network at the county, commune, and brigade levels of administration—has been an ingredient of China's economic program since 1958, the phenomenon has been little studied.

Chinese rationale for rural industrialization is both political and economic. On the one hand, policy makers emphasize the economic contribution these enterprises can make to rural communities — by expanding production, providing services and employment, and by cultivating industrial skills. On the other hand, these small-scale enterprises, in contrast to those in many other developing countries, do have an additional political purpose—to strengthen the collective economy in the interests of continuing the socialist transformation of the rural sector. More specifically, the political rationale is based on the

premise that industrial enterprises will eventually become
primary sources of income for the commune and brigade levels
of ownership. The ability to use such income to raise
agricultural productivity and to narrow disparities among
teams within brigades is a prerequisite to achieving a
political goal—the transition from team to brigade level
accounting. The dual nature of these enterprises has often
been controversial, the focus of both theoretical debates and
political struggles during China's policy oscillations. A
single stay during one specific political phase could only
have given me half of the picture of the actual development
of rural industries.

To the extent that establishment and operation of rural
enterprises are dependent on higher level institutional
support and control (e.g. in setting production plans and in
providing raw materials, marketing channels, and worker
training), an understanding of how such enterprises develop
also highlights aspects of the relationship between rural
communities and higher levels of administration. To analyze
these relationships, one needs in-depth information from
people involved at every level of the development
process—from provincial and country administrators who are
responsible for setting developmental policy to cadres and
workers at the commune and brigade levels who are responsible
for implementing that policy. Furthermore, rural industrial
enterprises require a new type of rural worker. Peasants who
have spent much of their life devoted to agricultural
production require new skills and new forms of work
discipline when transferred to labor in rural industries, and
the formation of a rural industrial labor pool in turn
introduces new forms of social stratification into rural
communities. To analyze both the frustrations and
aspirations of individuals situated differentially within the
changing socio-economic hierarchy, I needed a pool of
informants sufficiently large to reflect the complexity of
the effect of socio-economic change on individuals within the
local system. Again, while scholars conducting refugee
interviews may be sensitive to such complexities, they may be
unable to obtain informants appropriate to the task.

The Research Site

As a resident of Hong Kong, I have been able to take
advantage of standard arrangements to visit the Canton Delta
with a minimum of red tape. Such access has been expanded
and relaxed in recent years. Nearly all tourists can now
visit China through Hong Kong, although some tours continue
to be closely monitored. My own first visits began in the
summer of 1974. Several short trips were required to

pinpoint one site suitable in terms of accessibility and suitability to my research goals. Since the success of my fieldwork was dependent not just on finding the most appropriate type of commune but also on the degree of cooperation from its officials, being on the spot greatly facilitated site selection. After visiting several communes in the Canton Delta, I finally focused my interest and efforts on Huancheng commune in Xinhui county. Even my earliest "scouting expeditions" were by no means a waste of time. They still provided useful field materials.

I eventually chose Huancheng commune for several reasons. In terms of convenience, Huancheng is located between two important urban centers in the Canton Delta, and there is regular public transportation by bus and boat between them and Canton. The commune is thus quite accessible. I could travel there without too much official help or interference.

The choice of Huancheng was fortuitous for another reason. It is a "periurban commune" with close ties to state industrial complexes in the nearby urban centers of Jiangmen and Huicheng. Huancheng enjoys the benefits of concentrated material and human resources, thus supplying informants whose work and backgrounds were sufficiently varied.

Huancheng commune was an excellent choice for yet another reason. In China, personal ties, however far removed, do facilitate entry into the community, and in that regard, my mother's family origin in the area was useful. Cadres and other commune members welcome me now more or less as a native returning home for visits. My ability to use the local dialect certainly helped. To protect my informants and to allay suspicion, however, I found it important not to pursue local connections too eagerly. I kept a distance from my relatives until local cadres, learning about them, took the initiative to arrange for us to meet.

The primary reason I chose Huancheng commune, however, was that its characteristics allowed me to pursue the analytic problems upon which my research focused. I was convinced of the commune's suitability after two trips, during which I managed to survey different aspects of the commune and to become acquainted with the cadres with whom I would be working. Huancheng is not a "model" commune. Its industries are at once meshed with industry in the nearby urban centers and serve agriculture in the immediate area. Of particular interest to me was the fact that the area where the commune is located has long been known for handicrafts made from palm, a local cash crop. Some commune and brigade enterprises developed out of these handicrafts, and I felt that the transformation of traditional handicraft industries from private to collective ownership would be worth analyzing since so much of present development is intimately tied to the potentials as well as constraints posed by the past.

Furthermore, Huancheng commune has a three-tiered system of ownership—commune, brigade, and team—each with different ownership rights, material endowments, and political power. Brigades have had varying degrees of success in the development of rural enterprises. Because of my interest in the relationship between the development of rural industry and the possibilities for developing higher forms of collective ownership, it was important that one of Huancheng's 29 brigades had actually made the transition from team to brigade level accounting. In analyzing the relationship between production and ownership, a comparison between this brigade and others, the former presumably more politically advanced, has in fact been instructive. Due to problems surrounding the transition from team to brigade level accounting, the brigade was not mentioned to me until I had already gained a certain degree of trust from local cadres. When I finally did learn of this transition, I reorganized my research plan to give special attention to this particular brigade.

Since China is so vast and varied, I am aware, as are the other contributors to this volume, that research limited to a single case cannot provide an adequate basis for generalization. As Professor Fei Xiaotong also points out, China consists of millions of different communities situated in different regional contexts with unique historical configurations. However, a survey of the literature on Chinese rural development over the past several decades also reveals considerable continuity in general political guidelines, in concrete problems of policy implementation, as well as regularity in spatial patterns of development. By locating a commune in the spatial and temporal context of a regional system, according to the conceptual framework developed by G. William Skinner, the researcher is better able to evaluate its developmental potential and its response to various forms of political penetration. Thus, after several trips to the area surrounding Huancheng, I was comfortably able to classify that commune as a periurban commune in the core area of an agriculturally productive flood plain. While generalizations from Huancheng to other types of communes may be difficult, Huancheng may nonetheless be considered representative of other periurban communes in similar ecological circumstances.

Doing Research in Huancheng: Earliest Visits

By the time I formally approached the Chinese officials in Guangdong concerning my research, I had already gathered considerable information about my field site. During previous trips, I had pinpointed the locality, decided who I wanted to interview and which factories I wanted to study. I was also able to explain to Chinese authorities my reasons for selecting that site as well as my research hypotheses and procedures. As Pasternak and Butler have also indicated, this specificity served to reduce substantially the apprehensions provincial officials may have had about my work. When these officials contacted local cadres at the county and commune levels, moreover, they remembered me because of my earlier visits. They also felt "safe" discussing my project with me, because I entered the community to conduct research with the approval of higher-level authorities.

I started my data collection with what might be described as "standard" visits to commune officials and factories, in the course of which I learned something of the special characteristics of the commune's political economy. For instance, I was told about the stages through which socialist transformation and the commune's agricultural economy had passed. I was shown specific water conservation projects, learned about cropping patterns, and was told about differences in endowments and characteristics of the commune's constituent brigades and teams. Many of these "leads" were followed up during later visits. I was also able to visit every commune level factory and talk to their managers about the history and present operation of these enterprises.

The social landscape of the commune became clearer as I sat down with old farmers and reconstructed the ethnographic history of the area during pre-revolutionary times—the land tenure system, lineage organization, periodic markets, marriage patterns, village feuds, local bullies, and power relations. Old peasant activists who later became cadres also contributed their share to my understanding of the history of the area, describing the propaganda and mass organizational work they had done in the course of collectivization. They spoke of their motivation and enthusiasm during the 1950's, recalled the economic hardships and political fluctuations of the "three bad years" (1959-1961), and the difficulties during the period of the Cultural Revolution. They expressed uncertainties and reservations about certain policies as well as concern about a growing skepticism among the young. The stories they told me provided a human dimension that supplemented the more quantitative aspects of my research. Upon my return to Hong Kong, a substantial amount of what they told me could be further corroborated by documentary data.

Doing Research in Huancheng: Later Visits

I gathered most information necessary to my research during a second round of follow-up visits. I was then able to interview key persons and to acquire detailed information that had been impossible to obtain during my earlier official tours. Because I was able to depend upon an informal network of cadres and friends in the community, official interference from higher levels was minimal. I interviewed a wide range of people responsible for operation of the industrial complex linking brigade, commune, and county level enterprises, including commune and brigade accountants, factory managers, and a variety of workers employed in different types of enterprises. The content of these later interviews switched from discussion of abstract policy to the practical problems of implementation. At the same time, I was able to obtain some quantitatlve data illustrating qualitative relationships.

My ability to gather data was further enhanced by my willingness to assist the commune in solving some of its marketing and technical difficulties. They suggested that since I was interested in analyzing the successes and failures of the enterprises, I might also be interested in helping to make them work. They took the initiative to explain the necessity of obtaining contracts from overseas Chinese manufacturers (since these are officially sanctioned). They also explained their need for English teachers to train their technical personnel. Cadres and other commune members started to volunteer new areas that my research should cover: "Come visit our new printing workshop that took contracts from Southeast Asia." "Have you examined our new commercial enterprise—the commune tea house?"

My positive response to these suggestions created a new relationship and opened the way to new kinds of data. My hosts eventually began to involve me in the on-going processes of the community instead of merely treating me as a researcher gathering information.

Last but Not Final Round of Information Gathering: Quantitative Data

During my six years of contact with the commune (1976-1982), despite major changes in national policy toward rural communities, I found that personnel changed little. After 1978, however, the national turn toward more liberal policies became very obvious in the commune. Each time I returned, I found different policies with respect to the organization of production and redistribution. A new mentality developed corresponding with new ways of getting things done. Production policies which would have been unthinkable during late 1976 were being implemented in full force in 1980. I took the opportunity provided by the liberal political atmosphere to ask for a comprehensive set of statistical data on the commune and its enterprises. I found cadres willing to cooperate. Four years after the suppression of radical elements, most felt comfortable with the new liberal policies. Cadres are now quite eager to receive overseas support and to permit a technical analysis of development policies. Together we worked out statistical ways to evaluate the effectiveness of certain economic policies. We discussed potential sources of tension and grievances within the commune.

We continue to keep in touch. If the general political climate remains as flexible as it has been during the last four years, I can look forward to continuous and varied interaction with the commune. We have even discussed the possibility of proposing an extension of my study to higher officials in order to gather more cases for analyzing patterns of development.

Strengths and Weaknesses

I fully agree with Anne Thurston that given some of the current difficulties with academic exchanges, flexibility is a necessary virtue.[4] With the increasing autonomy of academic institutions and provincial level administrations, opportunities for a series of short visits should be followed up more seriously. These visits may seem superficial at first; but if one uses them wisely to accumulate data and to build up momentum for further opportunities, one may be amazed at how much data can be gathered. Each trip adds a piece to the whole.

But this type of research can be time consuming. For those who want to go to China for a year and then to write a book as quickly as possible, this form of research may not be

---

4. Anne F. Thurston and Jason H. Parker, "Introduction," in Anne F. Thurston and Jason H. Parker, editors, Humanistic and Social Science Research in China (New York: Social Science Research Council, 1980), p. 16.

appropriate. Moreover, not being able to remain in a community for long-term observation can be frustrating for anthropologists, many of whom choose to remain in the same place for as long as possible, both to observe full agricultural cycles and to benefit from sustained, continuing, daily contact with community members. But, on the whole, I would argue that multiple visits may prove more fruitful than one might expect.

Patterns of Commune and Brigade
Enterprise Development:
A Summary Report

Rural industrialization at the levels of the commune and brigade has been an integral part of the political economy of Chinese communes. The goals of rural industrialization, as noted in the preceding section, are both economic and political. First and foremost, Chinese leaders believe that rural small-scale industries are better able to support agricultural production than were the centralized, large-scale state industries of the past. Rural small-scale industries are closer to the markets they serve. They are also able to exploit local resources that, given the limitations of transportation and marketing in the Chinese countryside, would otherwise remain untapped. These enterprises can also be cost effective: their scale is small, the time involved in construction is short, and the technology required is usually simple. One might expect that the products of such small-scale enterprises might sometimes not be up to highest standards, but given the material conditions in the Chinese countryside, the provision and maintenance of expensive, sophisticated machinery could prove even more problematic.

Apart from the economic justifications the Chinese offer in support of rural industrialization, there are also social and political arguments. Rural industrial enterprises have never been intended to be totally self-reliant or locally oriented. If they have the potential, they are to be increasingly upgraded and integrated into state run industrial complexes. In this way, state industries will gradually transfer technology and industrial know-how to rural areas at a pace to which the latter can adjust. Such development is expected to draw the rural population into productive industrial employment and discipline and, in so doing, to broaden opportunities and outlooks. According to optimistic policymakers, the political goal of "narrowing the three disparities"—between town and countryside, industry and agriculture, and between mental and manual labor—will thus be furthered.

The Effects of Fluctuating Agricultural Policies:
Periurban and Peripheral Communes

A rural industrialization program that grows out of the rural political economy and caters specifically to it is intimately affected by fluctuating agricultural policies that filter down from the national to the local level. Agricultural economies at a regional core respond differently to changes in policy from those at the periphery. For example, the availability of raw materials and traditional crafts in an area growing cash crops stimulates the development of enterprises processing goods for wider markets. During a liberal policy phase, these enterprises can probably expect favorable institutional support and political direction from commune as well as from state commercial complexes. During a radical policy phase, however, the growing and processing of cash crops has often been criticized for being "speculative" and "profit oriented" and therefore for being a corruption of socialist ideals. As a result, not only is the supply of raw materials to these enterprises slowed during radical periods through the suppression of the growing of cash crops, but workers in these enterprises are often also dispersed to the fields. In addition, credit is usually limited and marketing opportunities reduced. Paradoxically, however, it has been precisely during such radical periods that rural-oriented enterprises (such as agricultural machinery stations) have been established by communes located in the regional periphery.

The Effects of Fluctuating Industrial Policies

Urban centers at every level of the regional system provide commune enterprises with a large market for products and services. They also supply surplus materials, training, and supervision. Through arrangements with urban complexes, therefore, periurban communes (such as Huancheng) have more favorable conditions for enterprise development than communes located in peripheral areas. The problem, however, is that state urban and commercial complexes are sensitive to changes in national policy. The fact that their fortunes correspond closely to policy phases also means that the fortunes of commune enterprises will also fluctuate. Because of their relatively isolated location, enterprises operated by communes in the regional periphery seem less sensitive to such shifts.

On the other hand, periurban communes are not necessarily better equipped for the development of rural enterprises. Cadres of the Xinhui County Bureau for Managing

Commune and Brigade Enterprises maintain that Huancheng is actually disadvantaged in several respects when compared with other, more peripheral, communes in the county. For example, with an unfavorable land-labor ratio, Huancheng lacks the land that would be needed to develop large-scale enterprises, such as a steel processing plant. Nor does it have the capacity to develop extractive industries (e.g. stone quarries or small coal mines) that would be needed to support large-scale plants. However, the commune maximizes its urban connections by concentrating on processing products for state factories and on manufacturing light industrial goods for the urban and export markets.

Let us take a closer look at the variety of enterprises in Huancheng and at how those enterprises have been affected by shifting policy cycles.

The Variety of Huancheng Commune's Enterprises

As of 1978, Huancheng commune had sixteen enterprises divided into two basic types—agricultural and industrial. Financing, planning, and supervision of these enterprises are handled by the Commune Office for Managing Commune and Brigade Enterprises.

Agricultural Enterprises. The seven commune level agricultural enterprises are oriented toward servicing agricultural production within the commune itself. Many of them were established by collectives during the 1950's and were then taken over by the commune when it was established in 1958. Initially, these agricultural enterprises were to provide teams with seeds, experimental cultivation techniques, and veterinary services. Their scale of operation has always been small. For example, a fish hatchery was established in 1959 with fewer than ten workers. It develops fish fry to sell to brigades in the commune at a low price, but its operation has never been entirely stable. In bad years, the hatchery has not even had enough fish fry to satisfy brigade demand.

The commune orchard was established during a liberal period in 1970, when 30 mu of land were acquired from one brigade to grow oranges and tangerines on an experimental basis. The goal was to revive a fruit growing tradition that had declined since the Japanese occupation. Although the commune has been subsidizing the project at a rate of 10,000 yuan a year, it is still too soon to know how successful it will be.

Despite their local orientation, even these agricultural enterprises reflect a sensitivity to national and regional policy phases. For example, an agricultural technology station was established during the radical phase of the Great Leap Forward. Since then it has responded to radical calls for reliance on indigenous technical ingenuity. The station has therefore organized young people for experiments in soil improvement, pest control, crop protection, and planting methods. The station's chief technician is a nationally known figure who, as a "peasant youth," relied on native ingenuity to develop new, improved rice strains for the prefecture. He also promoted the growing of winter wheat in this subtropical area of Guangdong in response to radical calls for paying primary attention to the cultivation of grain.

During more liberal phases such as the present, local enterprises cease to engage in experimentation. Instead, they are pressured by the commune administration to become as self-sufficient (and therefore as profitable) as possible. The commune is no longer prepared to subsidize these enterprises for the sake of aiding agriculture. Many local enterprises therefore are establishing urban connections and are beginning large-scale production for commercial units in Xinhui city. For example, the fish hatchery has expanded its fish breeding to the commune's numerous waterways (in order not to compete with agricultural land through the construction of fish ponds). Similarly, the orchard is now producing oranges for sale to export companies in Xinhui city. The commune timber farm at present employs 160 workers to produce bamboo, jute, pine, and oranges which it also sells to commercial units in Xinhui. Even the livestock and poultry farm, which was never run very efficiently as an experimental station, is now branching out into poultry production for export to Hong Kong.

As local enterprises respond to more liberal policies by orienting themselves to markets beyond the commune, they become increasingly subject to supervision by county level administrators. And county level supervision causes a new set of problems. For instance, Huancheng commune has had numerous conflicts with county administrators over pricing regulations and other marketing restrictions. One of the most common complaints from commune cadres is that county commercial units do not allow them to sell directly to export companies. Instead, the commune must sell its products to commercial units at a price fixed by the county, and commune cadres regard these prices as very low. As a consequence, production incentive suffers because commune members do not feel that they are accumulating sufficient profits. They are annoyed that the state commercial units pocket huge middleman fees—revenues that commune members feel should rightfully be theirs. Despite complaints, they also complain that county regulations and controls make it impossible for them to adjust flexibly to changes in market demand. The lopsidedness of power between the county and commune is obvious. There seems little that the commune can do. Norma Diamond is quite correct in her contribution to this volume in suggesting that local level leaders can be only as good as higher level county leaders allow them to be. She too notes that the development of village production is fundamentally dependent upon policies emanating from the county.

Industrial Enterprises. Huancheng Commune had nine industrial enterprises in 1978, and three new ones have been established since then.[5] These enterprises differ from brigade level enterprises as well as from each other in terms of their development priorities, service orientations, levels of technological sophistication, leadership and worker requirements, production and employment capacities, and higher level institutional supervision.

These enterprises can be divided into three categories. First, there are those servicing agricultural production and meeting local consumption needs. These are relatively small in scale, and their technological level is low. They do not often employ many workers and do not contribute a large output or profit to the commune.

Second, there are workshops that process local cash crops into consumer goods for urban and export markets. A typical example of this type of enterprise in Huancheng commune is the palm handicraft factory, which processes locally grown palm leaves into handicraft items for export to Europe and Southeast Asia. Although their technical requirements are not high, since most depend on handicraft skills, these enterprises do require substantial institutional support from county level commercial units for the distribution of their products. They also directly stimulate local agriculture by creating a demand for agricultural raw materials. Moreover, since their capacity for employment and for the accumulation of profits is large, they indirectly benefit team agriculture by providing employment and investment funds.

The third category includes enterprises which produce

5. In 1979, a plastic printing factory, a primitive workshop, and a knitting workshop were established in Huancheng Commune. The first two were helped by county factories, and the third relies on overseas Chinese capital and contracts.

parts or perform processing tasks for urban and state industries in the nearby urban centers. This type includes enterprises which depend on state resources to produce light industrial goods for the urban market. The paper factory at Huancheng commune is an example of this type of enterprise. Not only does this type require the highest level of technological sophistication of the three, but it also demands the strictest work discipline and training. Their institutional connections with higher level administration are most numerous, as they depend on the latter for state allocated production materials (such as fuel, metal, and chemicals), second hand machines, credit, and workers' training. Moreover, both their employment and accumulation capacities are large. Commune cadres are anxious to develop enterprises of this sort for economic as well as for social reasons. They provide funds for the commune to invest in agriculture and, at the same time, foster a more cosmopolitan, industrial orientation and outlook among commune members.

On the surface, the distribution of enterprises in Huancheng commune appears to be balanced among the three types. However, closer examination of the orientation and institutional context of these enterprises shows that most of them, even those which initially appear to be oriented most closely to the internal production needs of the commune itself, are closely tied to the urban and state industrial complexes.

For example, all the enterprises maintain a close relationship with their respective "coordinate units" in the county administration. The agricultural machinery station is paired with the County Agricultural Machinery Corporation, which fixes the station's standard of services and charges, supplies it with necessary fuel and machine parts, and trains its mechanics. The commune palm handicraft factory receives its production quota and necessary production materials directly from the County Native Products Export Corporation and the County Palm Handicraft Factory. Even the enterprise that is assumed to be the most locally oriented—the commune food processing factory—finds the prices it can set for its products strictly supervised by the County Food Grain Bureau in Xinhui city.

The dual orientation of these enterprises, downward to the commune's constituent brigades and teams and upward to the county, always creates a dilemma, especially for those enterprises supposedly servicing commune agriculture. For example, the agricultural machinery station and the agricultural machinery factory in Huancheng commune have been tempted to use their machinery for more profitable urban contracts instead of for manufacturing and repairing agricultural machinery for the commune's brigades. Instead of giving priority to building houses, pig sties, bridges, and canals for brigades, the construction team often takes contracts from the County Housing Authority to build houses in Xinhui city. The commune transport team has been accused of transporting goods for factories in Xinhui and Jiangmen instead of transporting needed seeds and fertilizers to the brigades. Most commune brick kilns are small-scale operations catering to rural building needs. But the new commune brick factory established in Huancheng in 1976 is one of the largest and most modernized in the county. The commune invested 400,000 yuan in the factory, which was based on a design provided by the Zhanjiang Fireproof Materials Factory. It depends on the County Materials Supply Bureau for a state allocated quota of coal and coal dust. Its production (10 million bricks a year) is sufficient both to satisfy the commune's needs as well as to meet some of the urban demand.

Regional Location and Policy Cycles

Norma Diamond, in her contribution to this volume, has suggested that the artificial severing of Taitou's ties with Qingdao has had a deleterious effect on the possibilities for Taitou's development. But if being a periurban commune has worked to the advantage of commune level enterprises in Huancheng, there have been disadvantages as well. The enterprises' dependence on urban subcontracts and export markets is somewhat "parasitic," and discourages commune enterprises from developing on their own initiative. Instead, they often find themselves pulled along by wider marketing concerns over which they have little control. Until they are more integrated into the state planning structure, they will always remain in the peripheral position of "taking the crumbs" from the state complexes.

Their ties with urban state structures make them particularly vulnerable to fluctuations in the wider political structure. During radical political phases, when rural self reliance is emphasized, both commune enterprises and their urban contractors are under pressure to sever mutually profitable ties. During liberal phases, inefficient state industries undergoing drastic trimming and reorganization readily drop their rural subcontracts on the periphery of the industrial structure. Detailed descriptions of enterprise development in Huancheng commune over the last 20 years display fluctuations corresponding to wider political cycles.

Logically, one can posit that the factors constraining or promoting industrial growth in communes located in the regional periphery are the opposite of those for periurban communes. During liberal phases, communes in the periphery suffer from a lack of connections that would stimulate the growth of enterprises. However, during radical phases, deliberate administrative directives often make units at each administrative level share with disadvantaged subunits what they have accumulated during the previous liberal period. While periurban units at every administrative level are allowed to maximize their material advantages during the next liberal period, peripheral units, though neglected to an extent, acquired a new material basis for development on their own during the preceding radical phase.

The Secular Trend of Development

Despite the fact that the economic development of Huancheng commune has been cyclical, tied to alternating patterns of radical and liberal policies, there has been a long-term, secular development of industrial enterprises, as both the enterprises themselves and the overall commune economy have gradually matured. Enterprises established during the early period of the commune enjoyed little initial investment. Their production capacity was small, and their direct or indirect effect on commune organization was slight. They employed few workers, and their demands for rural raw material were limited, and, since their technological level was primitive, they provided little modern industrial experience to their workers. Moreover, they accumulated little profit for the commune to invest in its rural units. As late as 1969, many of them had not been able to secure links with state complexes. Therefore, since they were unstable, they were especially likely to be closed down when state agencies consolidated for efficiency during liberal phases. They were also easily abandoned by urban contractors when the latter were under pressure to cut ties during radical political phases.

Since the early 1970's commune level administration in Huancheng has accumulated sufficient financial resources to build larger-scale enterprises. For example, the commune feels less economically constrained and has invested heavily in the commune's agricultural machinery station and in the brick factory. Many of the commune's enterprises have developed a steadily upward pattern of production, have stabilized their urban connections, and have gradually become an integral part of state complexes. To some extent, these connections will be more difficult to discard during radical phases and are more likely to be expanded during liberal phases. The paper factory is a good example. Despite humble beginnings, by the early 1970's the factory had been incorporated into provincial production plans. Despite the fact that it was criticized by radicals for being run by "technocrats," the factory has been able to maintain a steady output. During the last three years, more liberal policies have allowed the factory to update and modernize its machinery to meet the requirements of a more diversified production plan, more geared to the export market.

Some Recent Problems

Since 1979, commune level enterprises in Huancheng have been experiencing special difficulties. The problems seem to arise less from the complexities of management than from their production and marketing environments. Nationally, emphasis on the development of enterprises continues to be strong. Moreover, recent liberal policies have allowed a great deal of autonomy to commune enterprises, encouraging them to "exploit as much potential as they possibly can." Nonetheless, development efforts in Huancheng commune have been frustrated.

There seem to be two major bottlenecks. The first is related to the commune's agricultural economy. Following years of policy confusion, the rural sector has not grown sufficiently to create a genuine demand for the goods and services of commune enterprises. Cash crop production in particular suffered during the mid-1970's. However, the problems of agricultural stagnation were not apparent during the radical phase of 1973 to 1976, when administrators insisted that brigades develop a network of agricultural machinery repair facilities. To implement this policy, commune and county agricultural machinery factories were pressured to supply the necessary materials. However, some of the factories were unable to produce efficiently. As a result, the county government subsidized the inefficient production of substandard machines, which brigades were encouraged to buy with commune subsidies. Recent liberal policies do not allow such inefficient operations to continue. County administrations have discontinued the administrative support that created an artificial demand from the agricultural sector.

Secondly, the focus of state industrial complexes on more rational and efficient production plans has eliminated many of the commune's usual contractors. For example, the once famous Xinhui County Agricultural Machinery Factory, which manufactures hand tractors, has been pressured to close down some of its production because of high costs. State factories that survived the recent industrial reorganization have been pressured to give contracts to collective urban enterprises set up to take care of the city's unemployed. The less efficient commune enterprises have lost out in the race.

According to commune cadres, the next few years will be a difficult period for commune enterprises. With diminished demand from agriculture and urban industries, the commune is seeking capital and contracts from overseas Chinese in Hong Kong and Macao. Workshops have been set up to process items for these overseas manufacturers. However, this is a temporary measure until the domestic economy can regain its momentum. Because of its ties to overseas emigrants, Huancheng commune has been able to branch out in this new direction. How communes that do not have overseas ties will be able to break out of this difficult situation remains to be seen.

Furthermore, official sanctions for enterprise autonomy since 1978 have created conflicts between the commune and county administration. Commune cadres hint that the County Bureau for Managing Commune and Brigade Enterprises is increasingly concerned with urban unemployment. Consequently, the Bureau has blocked the commune from establishing profitable enterprises when commune enterprises have presented possible competition with county level enterprises.[6] The network of institutional support provided by the county administration for commune enterprises can easily be turned into an effective means of control. It is ironic that during the present liberal policy phase, when autonomy and initiative of lower collective levels are to be encouraged and respected, the power of the county over the commune has become even more apparent.

During my recent fieldtrip in the summer of 1982, I encountered skeptical responses from commune cadres over the national proposal for major changes in commune structure. In Huancheng, the issues were being discussed. Some cadres felt that if team agriculture and brigade enterprises were to be independent from the commune's political control, the commune enterprises would have no means to ensure raw material supply and market. Facing competition with county level state and collective enterprises, their already vulnerable situation would only worsen. For Huancheng commune, which must support seven thousand people who are not involved in agriculture, the picture in the near future appears grim.

---

6. In 1978, the commune proposed to establish a factory to process fruits and vegetables. The proposal was not accepted by the county bureau for fear that the enterprise might compete with county factories for raw materials.